MONOGRAPHS OF THE
SOCIETY FOR RESEARCH IN
CHILD DEVELOPMENT

SERIAL NO. 216, VOL. 52, NO. 2

SOCIAL PROCESSES IN
EARLY NUMBER DEVELOPMENT

GEOFFREY B. SAXE
STEVEN R. GUBERMAN
MARYL GEARHART

UNIVERSITY OF CALIFORNIA, LOS ANGELES

WITH COMMENTARIES BY
ROCHEL GELMAN AND CHRISTINE M. MASSEY
BARBARA ROGOFF

AND REPLY BY THE AUTHORS

MONOGRAPHS OF THE SOCIETY FOR RESEARCH IN CHILD
DEVELOPMENT, SERIAL NO. 216, VOL. 52, NO. 2

CONTENTS

ABSTRACT

SAXE, GEOFFREY B.; GUBERMAN, STEVEN R.; and GEARHART, MARYL. Social Processes in Early Number Development. With Commentary by ROCHEL GELMAN and CHRISTINE M. MASSEY and BARBARA ROGOFF; with Reply by GEOFFREY B. SAXE, STEVEN R. GUBERMAN, and MARYL GEARHART. *Monographs of the Society for Research in Child Development*, 1987, **52**(2, Serial No. 216).

The present study is an investigation of the interplay between social and developmental processes in children's numerical understandings in working- and middle-class home settings. Methods included interviews with 78 middle- and working-class 2½- and 4½-year-olds to assess their numerical understandings, interviews with the mothers about their children's everyday number activities, and observational studies of the mother-and-child pairs in interaction during prototypical number activities.

Our results provide evidence that the children in the study were regularly engaged with social activities involving number, though the nature of children's numerical understandings and their numerical environments differed in the following ways. (1) Younger children differed from older children in their numerical understandings across a variety of tasks that varied in their goal structure complexity: recitation of counting words, production of cardinal values for single arrays, numerical comparisons and reproductions, and arithmetic transformations. 4-year-olds from middle-class homes displayed greater competence on tasks with more complex numerical goals than did their working-class peers. (2) At home, variation in the complexity of children's everyday number activities paralleled our findings of age and social class differences in children's numerical understandings. (3) During mother-child teaching interactions, mothers adjusted the goal structure of a given activity to reflect their children's abilities to structure numerical goals, and children adjusted their goals to their mothers' efforts to organize the activity. In a minority of contexts, working-class mothers simplified the goal structure of the activity to a greater extent than did middle-class mothers. Overall, there were few differences between the middle- and working-class dyads in the complexity of numerical goals elaborated during interactions for children of equivalent age and ability.

These results support a model in which children's numerical environments are understood to be negotiated in their everyday activities—a negotiation that leads children's achievements to be linked at once to their own understandings and to the sociocultural context of their development.

PART 1
A COORDINATED APPROACH TO THE STUDY
OF CULTURE-COGNITION RELATIONS

I. THE PROBLEM

In this *Monograph*, we report an investigation of the interplay between social and developmental processes in children's cognitive development. A primary motivation for the study was to gain an understanding of the bases for a commonly reported association between children's social class and their cognitive achievements. Specifically, children from middle-class homes tend to outperform their working-class peers on measures of intellectual achievement (see White, 1982). We targeted our research toward relations between children's social class and their numerical understandings—a domain of cognition that we know young children use in their everyday lives and for which the character of developmental shifts is well documented.

To understand relations between social class and measures of numerical competence, we have investigated the everyday environments involving number with which children in middle- and working-class homes are engaged. We have conceptualized everyday environments as activity contexts actively negotiated by children and others. In this view, children contribute to the organization of their activities by generating numerical goals in accord with their current conceptualizations of these activities. Children's efforts to generate and accomplish numerical goals provide a context for them to construct new understandings. While children's activities may be independent ones, many of them are social, and it is the social context of children's number development that is our focus here. Other people, often parents, participate in structuring activities with children that are frequently more complex than those that children can construct on their own. These jointly constructed activities provide a context in which children may generate goals that differ from those that they would have created alone, and, thus, they may construct new understandings that are socially influenced.

To gain insight into the complex relations between children's developing numerical understandings and their jointly organized numerical activities, we have developed an analytic model that integrates social and developmental processes in the study of cognitive development. The model

3

entails three components: (1) a developmental analysis of children's numerical understandings, used as a basis to infer children's goals in everyday activities; (2) a cultural analysis of the goal structure of children's everyday number activities, used as a basis to assess children's everyday numerical environments; and (3) a social interactional analysis, used to assess the way children's goals emerge and shift in the course of adult-supported activity. We argue that a coordinated analysis involving each of these components is required for progress in understanding how children's developing numerical competence is interwoven with social forms of number representation and number activities.

The *Monograph* is divided into five parts. Part 1 is a presentation of the three-component approach and an overview of our methods. In Part 2, we present empirical analyses guided by our first component—developmental analyses of children's numerical understandings as a function of their age and social class groups. We report age and social class differences in children's competence and the nature of the numerical goals children appear to structure in their task solutions. In Part 3, we present results bearing on our second component—analyses of the social context of children's number development. We document the educational values mothers have for their children, and we analyze children's everyday cultural activities involving number, the activities with which their numerical goals are interwoven. In Part 4, we present analyses from our third component—social interactional analyses of the numerical environments that emerge during mother-child play with number activities. We report analyses of how the goals of mother and child emerge and shift during numerical activities and of how the emergent goal structure varies as a function of the children's age and ability levels, the dyad's social class, and activity complexity.

In Part 5, we conclude our treatment of social and developmental processes in early number development, showing how our three-component approach provides a basis for interpreting age and social class similarities and differences in early number development. We offer a critique of the construct of socially organized experience in models that address social processes in cognitive development and contrast our approach with other current models.

THE ANALYTIC MODEL

A guiding assumption of our treatment is that children's numerical understandings are their *goal-directed adaptations* to their numerical environments; therefore, the study of number development should entail coordinated investigations of children's emerging abilities to generate numerical goals and the shifting sociocultural organization of their numerical environments. Though we separate children's goals and their environments for analytic purposes, we consider them to be interwoven with one another, and we have adopted an interpretive framework that preserves their contextual properties.

A consideration of the following example serves to introduce the analytic dimensions of our approach. A mother engages her child with a common activity, setting the table for dinner. The mother puts plates on the table and then sends her child for the same number of knives, forks, and spoons. The child then attempts to accomplish the task as defined by the mother.

If we consider the child's goals in the activity, the child's ability to generate number reproduction goals enables his or her conceptualization of the numerical problem. The plates, knives, forks, and spoons have no inherent numerical properties, and no numerical relations involving equalities or inequalities inherently exist between these items. Numerical properties of these items and numerical relations between sets of items are generated only through the child's goal-directed activities of conceptualizing the items as countable and numerically comparable. Since, as we argue below, children's abilities to generate goals associated with a variety of numerical functions shift during the preschool years, analyses of children's abilities to generate numerical goals are necessary to gain insight into the nature of the numerical environments in which the child participates and into the understandings and the strategies he or she might generate in these activities.

If we consider the table-setting activity as a social environment, there are two levels at which the child's goals may be influenced. At a cultural level, everyday numerical activities and representational systems differ across culturally defined contexts. The problem structure of table setting as culturally defined (i.e., as an adult represents it) can be described as a numerical reproduction of a model set of elements (the plates). To achieve the superordinate reproduction goal, the child would have to structure and accomplish a number of subordinate numerical goals (e.g., the achievement of a numerical representation of the plates and then of the knives, forks, and spoons). As the child attempts to accomplish the culturally defined task, the task structure constrains and has implications for the child's goals and, consequently, the strategies the child generates. Moreover, insofar as the child attempts to use our counting system in the table-setting activity, the structure of this representational system (verbal signifiers for number with a base-10 organization) becomes interwoven with the task structure. For instance, during the activity, the plates may become "six" plates, a representation with properties that differ from an uncounted quantity (or from a representation generated with a numeration system that has a different organizational structure; for a discussion of cultural variations in numeration systems, see Saxe & Posner, 1983).

5

At a social interactional level, the adult may effectively alter the cultural activity by adjusting the goal requirements of the table-setting activity so that effective communication and mutual understanding are possible. For instance, during the mother's efforts to assist her preschooler, she may tell her child how many knives, forks, or spoons to get. As a result of her assistance, what was initially an activity that entailed the reproduction of one set (plates) with another (silverware) is now a task requiring a series of single-array numerical representations—an activity with a simpler goal structure.

In the remainder of this chapter, our purpose is to develop our first analytic component—an analysis of developmental shifts in children's numerical understandings. We also introduce our second and third components, showing how they are essential for a treatment of the interplay between social and developmental processes in children's understandings.

FIRST COMPONENT: THE INTERPLAY BETWEEN FORM AND FUNCTION IN CHILDREN'S EARLY NUMBER DEVELOPMENT

To examine the interplay between children's goals and their environments in early number development, we have adopted a perspective similar to that outlined by Werner and Kaplan (1963) in their general treatment of symbol formation. Werner and Kaplan distinguish between form and function, on the one hand, and between means and goals, on the other, two closely linked sets of constructs that differ essentially only in level of analysis. Functions and forms constitute intellectual capabilities (characteristics of mind, cognition, capacities, etc.), while goals and means are constructs restricted to a person's efforts to accomplish particular tasks.

As we use these terms, numerical functions and numerical forms are defined in relation to one another, as are goals and means. Numerical functions are the generalizable numerical uses to which forms can be put; examples of distinguishable numerical functions are the representation of single sets, the comparison/reproduction of sets, and arithmetic composition/ decomposition of sets. Numerical forms, on the other hand, are those symbolic constructions and problem-solving procedures that serve numerical functions; for instance, a counting strategy is a numerical form that serves the function of numerical representation. With respect to goals and means, the child attempting to set the table establishes goals associated with the function of number reproduction and generates means—specific numerical forms such as counting strategies—to accomplish these goals.

One of Werner and Kaplan's (1963) major contributions was their analysis of the interplay between form and function. They considered, for instance, the effect that an emerging linguistic function, such as denotative reference, has on the child's generation of novel linguistic forms (syntactic, pragmatic, and morphological). During infancy, gestural and intonational forms—early reaching, cooing, and babbling—have prelinguistic functions (e.g., grasping and affective expression). With the emerging function of denotation in early childhood, the child attempts to adapt his or her already acquired gestural and intonational forms (reaching and cooing) as means to accomplish goals associated with the new function (e.g., reaching while vocalizing to indicate that a parent attend to a particular object). Such prior forms are clearly limited in their ability to serve the purpose of the newly emerging denotative function, and the child gradually structures novel forms of a function-specific character. The process of construction passes through various transitional phases, such as the generation of onomatopoeic forms (as in "choo-choo" for "train") and, later, the generation of more clearly specialized syntactic and morphological forms (as in such expressions as, "Look at the train"). The child's generation of new forms reciprocally creates conditions for the emergence of new functions and novel goals. For instance, forms for denotative reference are a logical precondition for the self-regulation of behavior through speech in problem solving—labeling pieces with, "That's the smokestack," as the child tries to find a proper place for a piece in a train puzzle (cf. Vygotsky, 1962, and more recent extensions of this approach, e.g., Wertsch, 1986).

We have applied an analysis of form/function shifts to children's developing numerical cognitions.[1] Central to our definition of numerical function is the construct of "correspondence operation," a construct basic to both philosophical (Frege, 1884; Whitehead & Russell, 1927) and psychological definitions of number (Fuson & Hall, 1983; Gelman & Gallistel, 1978; Piaget, 1952, 1975; Resnick, 1982; Saxe, 1979; Wagner & Walters, 1982). In our analysis, numerical functions are rooted in children's understanding of correspondence operations. Consider, for instance, the function of number representation and the centrality of correspondence operations to the definition of this function. When a child uses the number word "five" (a form) to refer to five objects, this word has numerical significance insofar as it is used to signify (at least implicitly) a summation of numeral-to-object correspondences—either the summation of the positions of correspondences in an enumeration, as in "the fifth object" (ordinal number), or the summation of the correspondences themselves, as in "the five objects" (cardinal number). Shifts in children's understanding of correspondence operations are central to the emergence of numerical functions.

There are four principal numerical functions that emerge during the preschool years. These functions include denotative iterations (with number

[1] Greeno, Riley, and Gelman (1984) also offer a model in which children's goals are a central construct. While the Greeno et al. account does focus specifically on counting, it lacks the developmental focus central to the Werner and Kaplan (1963) account, a focus we find critical to understanding the interplay between social and developmental processes.

words; see Fuson & Hall, 1983; Fuson, Richards, & Briars, 1982; Gelman & Gallistel, 1978), representations of single sets (Fuson, Pergament, Lyons, & Hall, 1985; Gelman & Gallistel, 1978; Schaeffer, Eggleston, & Scott, 1974), reproduction/comparison of sets (Piaget, 1952; Saxe, 1977, 1979, 1981), and elementary arithmetic operations with sets (Brush, 1978; Carpenter & Moser, 1982; Cohen, 1984; Ginsburg & Russell, 1981; Klein, 1984; Starkey & Gelman, 1982). We argue that these functions compose a developmental sequence in that they differ with respect to the complexity of correspondence operations that each entails. Below, we describe the correspondence operations required by each of the four targeted numerical functions as well as shifts in form/function relations over the course of early number development.

Level 1: Denotative Reference and Nominal-enumerative Correspondences

Denotation is a common function in the very young child's speech, a function rooted in the child's understanding that words can be put in correspondence with objects. Such correspondence operations are evident when, for instance, a 24-month-old points to the family cat while exclaiming, "Cat!" and then to the sink faucet while saying, "Water." We argue that early number word use is also rooted in somewhat similar denotative correspondences. Consider the same child who assigns the number words "one, two, seven," to a 10-item collection while making a combination of playful pulsing gestures to elements and global sweeping gestures to segments of the array. Though some features of the 2-year-old's actions are characteristic of conventional number word use (the child counts fruit and toys with the same number words and consistently uses the same ordering of number words), there is little evidence that the 2-year-old originally uses these actions to establish one-to-one correspondences between number words and objects or that the child treats the last value of the enumeration as a numerical representation of the array.[2]

Empirical evidence that children use number words to serve a nominal/enumerative function and that this function antedates other numerical functions comes from various sources. In a study of children's knowledge of counting, Schaeffer et al. (1974) presented children with what they termed a "cardinality task." Children were presented with a set of five to seven elements to count. After the count, the array was immediately covered, and

---

[2] We recognize that there is a growing literature that documents infants' abilities to distinguish perceptually small sets (Antell & Keating, 1983; Starkey & Cooper, 1980; Strauss & Curtis, 1981; Van Loosbroek & Smitsman, 1986). These abilities, like early number word strings, may be important precursors to later emerging numerical forms and functions.

children were asked how many elements there were. Schaeffer et al.'s subjects, rather than responding with the last number word of their count, would often respond with a different number or repeat the last several number words just recited. These findings have been replicated in more recent studies of children's early number capabilities using tasks similar to the Schaeffer et al. task (Fuson et al., 1985; Markman, 1979; Wilkinson, 1984).

Though the denotative/enumerative function does not lead the child to produce numerical values, the emergence of this function creates conditions for the child's acquisition of cultural forms for number representation. (For documentation of shifts in number word sequence forms during the preschool years, see Fuson et al., 1982; and for a discussion of children's discovery of the base-structure organization of the string that extends through childhood, see Ginsburg, 1977; and Kamii, 1981.) As the child begins to accomplish goals associated with the more complex numerical functions discussed below, he or she draws the number word forms into efforts to achieve goals associated with those more complex functions, and, thus, these early emerging forms will take on novel numerical properties.

Level 2: The Representation of Single Sets and Summations of Correspondences

The representation of single sets is a function rooted in an implicit understanding that number word–to–object correspondences in a count can result in a summation rather than merely an enumeration of an array. A number of studies provide convergent evidence that young children use this numerical function. These include observations of children's spontaneous and appropriate reference to cardinal values in problem solving (Gelman, 1972), children's use of the last number word of a count to refer to cardinal values of sets (Gelman & Gallistel, 1978; Schaeffer et al., 1974), children's appropriate detection of counting errors (Briars & Siegler, 1984; Gelman & Meck, 1983; Saxe, Sadeghpour, & Sicilian, in press), and children's understanding that the number assigned to an object is dependent on its ordinal position in an enumeration (Gelman & Gallistel, 1978). These studies have revealed that, by 3 or 4 years of age, most children do use number words as numerical signifiers for single arrays and that they understand some logicomathematical properties of number words, at least for small set sizes. Gelman, Meck, and Merkin (1986) have argued that the development in children's understandings between 3 and 5 years can be understood as developments in children's strategies to represent arrays.

Evidence that young children are adapting and specializing strategies to achieve single-array goals is contained in a study by Shannon (1978). She presented 3–6-year-olds with configurations of dots (either seven, 10, or 14) arranged in three rows and asked children to count them. Younger children tended to count the dots haphazardly, counting the elements in proximity to one another rather than using a procedure that would minimize the possibility of skipping or double counting items. Slightly older children tended to use a strategy that followed the exterior form of arrays, reducing the probability of skipping but not of double counting some elements. Finally, the oldest children often used a strategy based on the linear arrangement of items, minimizing the possibility of double counting and skipping items. Sicilian (1985), in a study with blind children, has documented analogous developmental shifts in the blind child's construction of strategic forms involving the use of hands to scan and track elements to minimize double-counting and skipping errors.

There is evidence that children transform tasks with comparison/reproduction goal structures (level 3 in our sequence) into nominal enumerative (level 1) and single-array representation (level 2) goal structures. In a study of children's use of counting in problem solving, Saxe (1977) presented 3–6-year-olds with tasks that required numerical reproductions and comparisons of sets. In the reproduction tasks, the child was presented with a model set and was required to produce a numerical copy. In the comparison tasks, the child was required to compare numerically two sets that differed in value but had the same spatial extent. If children did not count spontaneously in either task, they were prompted, "Would counting help?" The youngest children generally appeared to form either nominal/enumerative (level 1) or single-set number representation (level 2) goals. Consistent with level 1 goals were simple recitations of number words with sweeping gestures over objects. Consistent with level 2 goals were counts of only one row or both rows continuously as if they were one.

In summary, the studies cited indicate that, by 3 or 4 years of age, children begin to represent the numerical values of single arrays. To accomplish goals associated with this novel function, the young child makes an effort to assign one and only one number word to each element in a count, a behavior pattern in which the child incorporates previously acquired number word sequences. Thus, old forms are deployed to serve a newly emerging numerical function. With the child's generation of values for single sets, he or she creates conditions in which the relation between representations of more than one array may be considered, a function that follows in development the representation of single arrays.

Level 3: Comparing and Reproducing Summations of Correspondences

The comparison/reproduction function of number word forms is based on an understanding not only that correspondences can be directed toward objects but also that the products of two sets of numeral-to-object correspondences can be compared. Goals of numerical reproduction and comparison are evident in such activities as setting the table and comparing number of candies with a friend.

Children's generation of forms to achieve numerical reproduction goals was documented in older children by Saxe (1977). When presented with a numerical reproduction task, some 4-year-olds seemed to conceptualize the goal of the task as a numerical reproduction; yet they did not generate strategies to accomplish the reproduction systematically. Instead, they appeared to adapt a single-array representation strategy to accomplish the task in a trial-and-error fashion: first they counted the available set; next they counted the model; and then, through a process of additions, subtractions, and recounts, they equalized the model and the copy. Six-year-olds often generated more specialized strategies to serve the number reproduction function, typically counting the model and then counting the same number from the available set to make their copy.

Evidence that children's use of the single-array and the comparative/ reproduction functions (levels 2 and 3) antedates the arithmetic function (level 4) comes from analyses of children's counting strategies to solve elementary arithmetic tasks (e.g., Carpenter & Moser, 1982; Cohen, 1984; Fuson et al., 1982; Groen & Parkman, 1972; Steffe, Thompson, & Richards, 1982). When presented with an arithmetic task such as "Wally had 3 pennies. His father gave him 5 more pennies. How many pennies did Wally have altogether?" (Carpenter & Moser, 1982, p. 14), some younger children appear to construct level 2 or 3 goals. They count to some term without a clear indication of trying to compose two distinct representations, or they count the two sets separately but do not attempt to compose the two terms.

Level 4: Relating and Manipulating Summations of Correspondences in Arithmetic Reasonings

Arithmetic reasonings are more complex than the reasonings that underlie level 3 goals: they entail not only generating and/or considering two numerical values (level 3) but also an operation of composition or decomposition of two values.

Many studies have documented shifts in strategic forms children use to solve arithmetic word and computational problems (for a review, see Carpenter & Moser, 1982). The most common forms are counting strategies. Various researchers (e.g., Carpenter & Moser, 1982; Fuson, 1982) have shown that, when children are presented with arithmetic problems such as "Wally had 3 pennies . . . ," they deploy a "counting all" strategy: they begin by counting from one the first term of the problem (often on the fingers) and then continue with the second term of the problem. Older children use a "counting on" strategy, a more sophisticated adaptation of counting to the arithmetic goal: they add the second array to the first by counting on from the value of the first array. Children's early use of counting to solve elementary arithmetic problems is an indication that children are adapting forms elaborated to serve the earlier emerging functions of single- and double-array number representations to serve the novel arithmetic function.

The use of counting procedures to solve arithmetic problems is not unique to children raised in Western settings—settings that often place a high value on early mathematical skills. In comparative studies with a Papua New Guinea group that traditionally uses a body-part counting system with no base structure, Saxe (1983, 1985) documented similar shifts in individuals' use of the body system to solve novel arithmetic problems that are emerging as a function of their contact with the West.

Individuals generate more specialized arithmetic problem-solving strategies such as the carrying and borrowing algorithms associated with school contexts and regrouping strategies associated with out-of-school contexts (Carraher, Carraher, & Schliemann, 1985; Lave, 1977; Posner, 1982; Saxe, 1987). Since these strategy types go beyond those common to the age range of children in our sample, we do not review them here.

THE SHIFTING ORGANIZATION OF CHILDREN'S NUMERICAL GOALS

While the four targeted functions can be ordered with respect to their logical complexity and tend to emerge in sequence, we hasten to qualify our claim for sequentiality. Aspects of children's activities such as the set size of arrays influence the functions children use (Coburn, 1983; Fuson & Hall, 1983; Gelman & Gallistel, 1978; Piaget, 1952; Saxe & Mastergeorge, 1986; Siegler, 1986; Siegler & Robinson, 1982; Winer, 1974). Thus, owing to problems that are specific to larger sets, a 4-year-old may generate a single-array number representation goal with a small set but a nominal/enumerative goal with a larger set in otherwise identical number representation tasks. Early number development is inherently multileveled: children are adapting and specializing forms to serve a number of distinct functions during the same time period. Indeed, some forms may be undergoing processes of specialization to serve higher-level functions with smaller sets, while other forms may be only newly incorporated to serve less complex functions with larger sets. In the empirical studies that follow, we attempt to gain insight into the interplay between the child's elaboration of multiple numerical forms and functions and their participation with socially organized number activities in their everyday lives.

CULTURAL (COMPONENT 2) AND SOCIAL-INTERACTIONAL (COMPONENT 3) PROCESSES IN CHILDREN'S FORMATION OF NUMERICAL GOALS

Children's numerical goals emerge in their everyday numerical activities, activities that are often socially organized. Understanding the role of social processes in children's numerical goals requires both analyses of the goal structure of the numerical activities with which children are engaged (component 2) and analyses of how the goal structure of these activities emerges over the course of social interactions between children and adults or more capable peers (component 3). These analyses will provide insight into how children's goals are influenced by the sociocultural contexts of their development.

Though there have been numerous efforts to treat social processes in children's intellectual development, such efforts generally fall short of our targeted concerns. The studies that exist tend to examine only the effects of environmental variables on children's cognitive achievements. Lacking a concern with the character of children's goals and the way these goals take form in social activities, these treatments fail to provide analyses of the interplay between social and developmental processes in children's generation of numerical goals and, hence, their developing numerical understandings.

We review prior research on social class differences in children's cognition in Parts 3 and 4 of the *Monograph* prior to presenting our results. In Part 3, we stress the need for investigation of the number activities with which children are engaged. We then offer a conceptual analysis of the goal structures of our subjects' activities that parallels our treatment of the emergence of the four numerical functions in early number development. Thus, we categorize activities into those involving nominal enumerations, the cardinal/ordinal representation of values, the comparison/reproduction of values, and arithmetic. We also report mothers' educational values and educational aspirations for their children, which we had assumed might differ across the social class groups in the study.

In Part 4, we review the existing literature on social interaction and early cognitive development, and we argue for social interactional analyses of the goals that emerge during adult-child play with number activities. We then undertake detailed analyses of adult-child interactions during prototypical number activities to determine how goals emerge and shift. We describe both the ways that adults adjust the goal structure of numerical activities to children and the ways that children may adjust their goal-directed activities given the directives of an adult. We argue that the goal structure of numerical activities emerges through reciprocal adjustments of mother to child and child to mother, adjustments that lead to a numerical environment linked both to the understanding of the child and to the culturally defined activity.

II. OVERVIEW OF METHODS

This chapter contains a general description of our subject populations as well as an overview of our procedures and administration schedule. In subsequent chapters, we present each procedure in detail.

SELECTION OF SUBJECTS

Recruitment.—Dyads were recruited through a variety of sources, including Head Start programs, local fairs, and church organizations. On first contact, potential subjects were informed that the purpose of the project was to find out what children might be learning about numbers in the home setting and that they would be paid for their participation. Interested mothers were then interviewed (generally at some later date) to determine whether they met the selection criteria outlined below. All dyads who participated in the project were paid $25 plus necessary carfare and baby-sitter fees.

Selection criteria.—All mother-child dyads in our sample met the following criteria. (1) All dyads were members of either a "middle-class" or a "working-class" family. We used the Duncan 99-point scale to define these classes (Duncan, 1961). In this procedure, we evaluated both parents' occupations on the Duncan scale and used the highest rating as an index of socioeconomic status. We defined our middle- and working-class populations as occupying a range of 45–92, and 6–34, respectively. (2) Children's ages were within either 30–38 months ("2-year-olds") or 46–60 months ("4-year-olds"). (3) All dyads were members of "intact" families, meaning that all fathers resided at home. (4) All dyads were Caucasian. We restricted race so that any inferences about social class could not be confounded with possible inferences about race. (5) All but a few dyads were from the same locality, Bay Ridge, a community in Brooklyn, New York. The remaining dyads were from an adjacent community. Bay Ridge itself is largely Caucasian and is composed of working- and middle-class families.

15

TABLE 1

FAMILY CHARACTERISTICS OF DYADS IN OUR SAMPLE

GROUP	DYADS (N)	DUNCAN SES M^a	SD	FATHER'S EDUCATION M^b	SD	MOTHER'S EDUCATION M^b	SD	MOTHER EMPLOYED (%)
2-year-olds:								
Middle class	20	66	14	14.9	2.9	13.8	2.1	15
Working class	18	18	7	11.6	1.0	12.0	.6	6
4-year-olds:								
Middle class	20	63	14	14.5	2.7	13.6	2.2	10
Working class	20	19	8	11.2	1.4	11.7	1.4	5

	CHILD'S AGE M^c	SD	CHILD'S SEX (% Male)	FIRSTBORN (%)	SIBLINGS (N) M	SD	PRESCHOOL ATTENDANCE (%)
2-year-olds:							
Middle class	33.8	2.1	65	20	1.1	.7	15
Working class	32.5	2.3	39	22	1.3	1.1	22
4-year-olds:							
Middle class	54.8	3.4	40	15	1.2	.8	60
Working class	53.1	3.9	45	15	1.4	.9	75

[a] The Duncan scale has a range of 1–99.
[b] Number of years in school. High school completion = 12, B.A. = 16, etc.
[c] Age in months.

DEMOGRAPHIC CHARACTERISTICS OF SAMPLE

Table 1 contains descriptive statistics on various characteristics of our population. Levels of education differed across social class for both fathers, $F(1,74) = 44.6$, $p < .001$, and mothers, $F(1,74) = 22.1$, $p < .001$, but not across age within social class for either fathers or mothers. Few mothers from either social class were employed. Though we attempted to balance the distribution of children's sex in our sample, we were not entirely successful. In particular, the 2-year-old middle-class population contains 13 boys and seven girls, whereas the 2-year-old working-class population contains eight boys and 10 girls. The number of firstborn children and of siblings is equally distributed over social class and age. Though the 4-year-old sample attended preschool to a greater extent than did the 2-year-old sample, there was no significant difference in preschool attendance as a function of social class at either of our two age levels.

OVERVIEW OF PROCEDURES

In addition to the time spent on the initial recruitment interview, each dyad participated in the project for 2–3 hours partitioned into two sessions—one at home and the other at a private elementary school in the community.

Home sessions.—The first meeting was conducted in the dyad's home. During this visit (after an initial greeting and warm-up period), both mother and child were interviewed separately by two members of the project staff, one male and the other female. During this visit, the child played with one staff member and was then interviewed by that staff member with a set of number assessment tasks or "games" (reported in Chap. III). These tasks included children's ability to recite the number word sequence, object counting, knowledge of elementary cardinal understanding, and elementary arithmetic. During the same period of time, the mothers were interviewed about their attitudes toward preschool learning achievements and their aspirations for and expectations about their children's educational and occupational careers (Chap. IV) as well as about the kinds of numerical activities with which their children were engaged in the home setting (Chap. V).[3]

Laboratory sessions.—Within the week following the first session (usually the next day), mothers and children were interviewed a second time at a local church-related school that had two large rooms available for videotaping and additional interviews. During this session, children were administered additional number-assessment procedures, a complex object-counting task, and a number reproduction task (Chap. III). Mothers and children were then videotaped as the mothers attempted to teach the children the complex counting task (Chap. VI) and the number reproduction task (Chap. VII). Mothers were also administered an interview in which they described the shifting character of their play on selected number activities over time (Chap. VIII).

---

[3] An initial questionnaire was mailed to the mothers selected for the study; the questionnaire was designed to facilitate the interview by prompting mothers to consider beforehand the kinds of number activities they played with their children.

PART 2
FIRST COMPONENT:
DEVELOPMENTAL SHIFTS IN
CHILDREN'S NUMERICAL UNDERSTANDINGS

III. THE NUMERICAL UNDERSTANDINGS OF CHILDREN IN OUR SAMPLE

Our analysis of form-function shifts in early number development in Part 1 provides a framework to assess age and social class differences in children's developing numerical understandings. We expected that younger children would display competence with numerical tasks that involved less complex numerical functions (e.g., nominal enumerations) but not with tasks that involved more complex numerical functions (e.g., numerical reproduction, arithmetic) and that, by 4½ years, children would display competence with the more complex functions.

We also expected social class differences on the basis of prior research on cultural factors in number development. In the comparative literature on number development, researchers have demonstrated that children in low-SES families tend to lag behind their middle-class peers on various dimensions of numerical knowledge (e.g., Kirk, Hunt, & Volkmar, 1975), though the extent of these social class differences has varied with the flexibility of the interview methods employed (Ginsburg & Russell, 1981). The cross-cultural literature also contains evidence of the association between cultural factors and number development: research on a range of Piagetian tasks has demonstrated different rates of emergence of number-related understandings (Dasen, 1972; Piaget, 1966) as well as cultural differences in the strategies and representational systems used for solving numerical problems (Saxe & Posner, 1983).

Children's numerical understandings were assessed with a battery of tasks selected on the basis of several considerations. We included tasks that spanned a wide range of numerical competencies that emerge during the preschool years. Some of these tasks were procedures adapted from Ginsburg & Russell's (1981) study of social class and early number development. For some, but not all, of these tasks, Ginsburg and Russell had found social class effects. Other tasks are widely used assessments in the number-development literature. We also assessed children's unassisted solutions to the complex counting and number reproduction tasks subsequently used in our analyses of mother-child interactions (reported in Chaps. VI and VII). For these two tasks, our objective was to provide analyses of the goals and solution strategies that children structured on their own in order to determine the ways children's goals and solution strategies might be altered when they were assisted by their mothers.

METHOD

Procedures

Children were interviewed in two sessions, first at home and then within 1 week at the school facilities. Each interview session lasted about 15–20 min. Prior to each session, the interviewer engaged children in play with finger puppets as a warm-up. All tasks were administered in a constant order; however, within a particular task type, we randomized or counterbalanced the set-size conditions as indicated below. Children's performances on the tasks administered in the home setting were audiotaped, and children's performances on the two tasks administered at the school facilities were videotaped (number reproduction and complex counting). A description of the individual tasks is presented below.

Counting words.—The purpose of this task, adapted from Ginsburg and Russell (1981), was to determine how far children could recite the counting words in the conventional order. Ginsburg and Russell reported an effect for social class on this task for preschoolers in their sample. In our adaptation, the interviewer presented a puppet to the child and said, "I want you to count as high as you can for [puppet's name]. You count while I tap on the drum for him." The interviewer followed a cadence generated by the child. This task was repeated once, and the highest number the child achieved without violating the conventional number word order was used as our measure of the child's knowledge of number words.

Comparative number judgments.—The purpose of this task, also adapted from Ginsburg and Russell (1981), was to assess children's knowledge of the order relation between pairs of number words. Ginsburg and Russell reported an effect for social class on this task for preschoolers in their sample. The interviewer presented the child with a puppet and said, "[Puppet's name] wants to know which number is bigger. Tell which number is bigger, *x* or *y*." The following *x, y,* pairs were randomized for each child: three, two; five, two; nine, six; seven, six; 10, five; three, four; three, six; five, eight; seven, eight; and six, 11. The number words in each individual pair were administered in the indicated order. The child's score was computed by counting the number of times the child produced a correct judgment.

Reading numerals.—The purpose of this task was to assess children's ability to recognize written numerals. The interviewer presented the child with a puppet and said, "[Puppet's name] would like to know what these numbers are. Would you please read them for him? What is this number?" The following numerals were presented for each child in random order: two, three, four, six, seven, eight, nine, 12, 15, and 27. The child's score was computed by counting the number of times the child produced a correct judgment.

Order invariance.—The purpose of this task, adapted from Baroody (1979), Gelman and Gallistel (1978), and Ginsburg and Russell (1981), was to assess children's understanding that an array can be counted in different orders and that each order yields the same value. We administered the task at two levels of set size, three and six elements. The interviewer presented the child with a card containing either three or six pictures of animals and said, "I want you to tell me how many animals there are. Let's count them starting with this one." The interviewer pointed to an animal at the child's extreme left, and the child counted. The interviewer then said, "You got *x* animals counting this way, from this end to this end [indicating the direction of the child's count]. How many animals do you think there would be if you counted this way and made this animal number 1 [the interviewer made a motion to the animal on the child's right and then covered the array]?" Following the child's response, the interviewer uncovered the array and asked, "How many animals do you think there would be if you made this one number 1 [as she indicated the middle item and then covered the array]?" The child was assigned a score of 1 for each correct judgment (the same cardinal value as produced in the prior count).

Cardinality.—The purpose of this task, adapted from various previous studies, including Gelman and Gallistel (1978), Ginsburg and Russell (1981), and Schaeffer et al. (1974), was to assess children's knowledge that the last number word recited in a count can be used to signify the value of an array. Ginsburg and Russell reported an effect for social class on this task. We administered this task at four levels of set size: two, three, seven, or nine elements. The interviewer placed a board containing either two, three, seven, or nine pennies and one puppet in front of the child. The board was made with a flap so that the pennies could be screened from the child's view during the task. The interviewer then said, "Here is [puppet's name] with some pennies [as she unfolded the board with a linear array of pennies inside]. I want you to count [puppet's name]'s pennies." After the child completed a count, the pennies were screened from the child's view with the flap. The child was then asked, "So, how many pennies does [puppet's name] have on his board?" For each correct judgment (repetition of last number word of count), the child was assigned a score of 1. In addition, for each accurate count a child produced on the four counting trials on this task, the child was assigned a score of 1 point. This value was added to the sum of

23

the two counting trials on the order invariance task to produce a "counting accuracy" score (which ranged from 0 to 6).

Elementary arithmetic.—Two tasks were used to assess children's knowledge of adding one to and subtracting one from a set.

a) Addition of one following cardinality question.—The purpose of this task was to provide an index of children's knowledge of the addition of one to a hidden set of a known quantity. Immediately following each trial of the cardinality task, the interviewer removed the screen and said, "Before, [puppet's name] had two/three/seven/nine pennies [correcting the child if he or she was incorrect]; now he's going to put another penny on his board." The interviewer turned the board so that the raised flap prevented the child from seeing the array inside. The interviewer then picked up a penny and showed the child that she was placing it on the board. The interviewer then closed the flap and put the puppet on top of the flap. The interviewer then said, "[Puppet's name] put another penny on his board. How many pennies does [puppet's name] have now?" The child was assigned 1 point for each correct response.

b) Addition and subtraction of one.—The second arithmetic task was adapted from Baroody (1979) and Ginsburg and Russell (1981). Ginsburg and Russell reported no effect for social class, but they did report an effect for race in their sample. We administered the task in each of the four following conditions: 4 + 1, 3 − 1, 3 + 1, and 4 − 1. In the 4 + 1 condition, the interviewer placed four pennies in a horizontal row in front of the child next to a puppet and placed three pennies in an available set next to the child. The interviewer then said, "[Puppet's name] wants to buy some ice cream/lollipops/gum/cookies, so I gave him four pennies. But wait; [puppet's name] says he really needs five. Can you fix his pile of four so it really has five?" The task was repeated for the other three conditions. For each correct judgment, the child received a score of 1. Each child was assigned a combined total arithmetic score consisting of the child's total score for this task plus his or her score on the addition of one following cardinality question task.

Complex counting.—The purpose of this task, adapted from Shannon (1978), was to assess the strategies children used to produce a count of a particular spatial configuration of elements. The interviewer presented the child with the array of five or 13 dots contained in Figure 1. The interviewer said, "I want you to count the dots and touch each dot as you count it." We created a coding scheme (presented in our results section below) to assess children's performances that is based on Shannon (1978) and on our observations of children's performance on our adaptation of the task.

Number reproduction.—The purpose of this task, adapted from Saxe (1977, 1979), was to assess children's strategies to reproduce numerically a model array of elements. We administered this task to each child at two

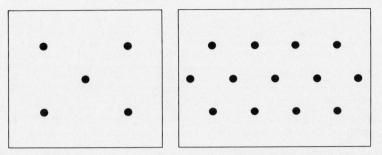

Fig. 1.—Set size 5 (left) and set size 13 (right) configurations for the complex counting tasks.

levels of set size, three and nine elements. The interviewer placed an available set of 15 pennies 3 feet to the left of the child. The interviewer then said, "Here are two friends, [name of puppet 1] and [name of puppet 2]. Let's put [puppet 1] right here with his pennies." The interviewer placed the first puppet 18 inches to the right of the child and a model set of three or nine pennies in front of the puppet. "Now let's put [puppet 2] over here." The second puppet was placed on a large piece of white cardboard in front of the child. "Go get [puppet 2] the same number of pennies that [puppet 1] has and put them in front of [puppet 2]." The interviewer pointed to the model set and then to the piece of cardboard in front of the second puppet.

RESULTS

Table 2 contains children's mean scores for all but the complex counting and number reproduction tasks (which will be analyzed in the subsequent section), and Table 3 contains the results of 2 (age) × 2 (SES) ANOVAs on children's performances. Even the 2-year-olds displayed numerical competence, as indicated by the mean counting word scores of 5.1 and 5.3 for the middle-class and working-class 2-year-olds, respectively. The 4-year-olds performed at higher levels across all but one of our measures, the order invariance task. The order invariance task was too difficult for children in all our population groups, and we did not observe much variability in children's performance on this task. (One possible reason for the low level of performance was the manner of task presentation. Recently, Gelman et al., 1986, have shown that, with minor variations in instructions, children's performances improve.)

There were two significant social class effects. Middle-class children performed at significantly more advanced levels than did working-class children on both the cardinality and the elementary arithmetic tasks. Age × SES interactions on the counting words task ($p < .10$), reading numerals

TABLE 2

CHILDREN'S NUMBER ACHIEVEMENT SCORES AS A FUNCTION OF SOCIAL CLASS AND AGE

TASK	MIDDLE CLASS		WORKING CLASS	
	M	SD	M	SD
Counting words:				
2-year-olds	5.1	4.1	5.3	4.0
4-year-olds	18.6	9.2	13.8	6.2
Comparative number judgments (10):				
2-year-olds	3.3	2.1	3.5	1.7
4-year-olds	6.4	2.6	4.9	1.9
Reading numerals (10):				
2-year-olds	1.2	1.9	1.4	1.8
4-year-olds	6.4	2.6	4.6	2.8
Order invariance (4):				
2-year-olds	.8	1.1	.9	1.0
4-year-olds	1.4	1.4	1.0	1.0
Counting accuracy (6):				
2-year-olds	1.2	1.4	1.4	1.3
4-year-olds	5.0	1.1	4.3	1.8
Cardinality (4):				
2-year-olds	.5	.6	.4	.7
4-year-olds	2.8	1.1	1.9	1.4
Arithmetic (8):				
2-year-olds	1.0	.8	.8	1.4
4-year-olds	5.2	2.3	3.2	2.2

NOTE.—Values in parentheses indicate highest possible score.

TABLE 3

F VALUES FOR CHILDREN'S ACHIEVEMENT SCORES AS A FUNCTION OF AGE, SOCIAL CLASS (SES), AND AGE × SES

TASK	FACTOR[a]		
	SES	Age	Age × SES
Counting words	2.7	59.0***	3.2
Comparative number judgments	2.04	23.2***	3.4
Reading numerals	2.2	61.7***	3.4
Order invariance	.5	1.2	.7
Counting accuracy	.8	113.8***	2.2
Cardinality	4.8*	68.6***	2.9
Arithmetic	8.2**	64.4***	4.8*

[a] For each F value, $df = 1,74$.

* $p < .05$.

** $p < .01$.

*** $p < .001$.

task ($p < .10$), comparative number judgments task ($p < .10$), cardinality task ($p < .10$), and elementary arithmetic tasks ($p < .05$) reflect the fact that, even though the 4-year-olds were more advanced in both social class groups, there was a more pronounced age difference in the middle-class as contrasted to the working-class groups.

Complex Counting Task

Accuracy.—We computed three indices of children's counting accuracy for each of the two set-size levels (five and 13). The first index consisted of a conventional definition of accuracy: the absolute difference between the last number word of the child's count and the actual number in the set (the higher the score, the less accurate the count). Two plausible difficulties with this index are that children might use a number list that is stable (in the sense that they use the same sequence with considerable regularity), but not conventional, and that they might focus on establishing one-to-one correspondences between pointing gestures and objects but not coordinate these gestures with their recitation of number words. Fuson and Hall (1983) and Gelman and Gallistel (1978) report cases of such behavior in young children. We therefore used two additional indices: we assigned children scores on the basis of the absolute difference between (1) the number of number words the child recited in the count and the actual number of dots in the array ("sequence") and (2) the number of the child's pointing gestures and the actual number of dots in the set ("correspondence").

Table 4 contains the mean accuracy scores of children in our sample for the three accuracy indices. A 2 (age) $\times$ 2 (SES) $\times$ 2 (set size, repeated) ANOVA was performed on each index. Each analysis yielded the same pattern of effects, consisting of main effects for age (last number word: $F[1,74] = 52.22, p < .0001$; sequence: $F[1,74] = 66.09, p < .0001$; correspondence: $F[1,74] = 43.53, p < .0001$), set size (last number word: $F[1,74] = 94.87, p < .0001$; sequence: $F[1,74] = 114.50, p < .0001$; correspondence: $F[1,74] = 93.99, p < .0001$), and an age $\times$ set size interaction (last number word: $F[1,74] = 15.29, p < .0005$; sequence: $F[1,74] = 32.62, p < .0001$; correspondence: $F[1,74] = 21.02, p < .0001$). Four-year-olds were more accurate than 2-year-olds, both groups were more accurate on the small than they were on the large set size, and the 2-year-olds' performance more closely approximated the 4-year-olds' performance on the smaller as opposed to the larger set-size condition. We found no social class effects.

Strategies.—Our strategy analysis was guided by Shannon's (1978) study. Shannon identified three basic strategy types. A proximal strategy was defined as a counting strategy based on "the proximity of items" (p. 1213), a peripheral strategy was defined as a strategy based on the exterior form of the array, and a linear strategy was defined as a strategy based on the linear

TABLE 4

MEANS FOR THREE INDICES OF COUNTING ERRORS ON THE COMPLEX COUNTING TASK
AS A FUNCTION OF SOCIAL CLASS AND AGE

	MIDDLE CLASS			WORKING CLASS		
AGE GROUP	Last Word	Se- quence	Corre- spondence	Last Word	Se- quence	Corre- spondence
Set 5:						
2-year-olds:[a]						
Mean	2.95	2.50	2.20	2.83	2.55	1.94
SD	1.99	2.40	1.96	2.18	2.41	2.18
4-year-olds:[b]						
Mean	.25	.25	.25	.20	.05	.0
SD	1.12	1.12	1.12	.52	.22	.0
Set 13:						
2-year-olds:[a]						
Mean	9.20	8.95	8.60	8.06	8.28	6.72
SD	4.05	4.16	4.57	4.35	4.35	4.68
4-year-olds:[b]						
Mean	2.90	2.40	2.45	2.45	1.60	1.80
SD	4.59	3.15	3.32	3.63	3.03	3.21

NOTE.—"Last Word" is the absolute difference between the actual number in the array and the last number word of the child's count. "Sequence" is the absolute difference between the actual number in the array and the number of sequence words of the child's count. "Correspondence" is the absolute difference between the actual number in the array and the number of the child's correspondence gestures to objects in the child's count.

[a] N = 20 (middle class) and 18 (working class).

[b] N = 20 (middle class) and 20 (working class).

arrangement of items. We had difficulty in applying the scheme as presented in Shannon's (1978) article, and, consequently, we elaborated her scheme to include seven categories. Since we did not observe variability in children's strategies on the set 5 condition, we applied the scheme only to the set 13 condition.

Table 5 contains our strategy codes for the set 13 condition. Two coders independently evaluated 16 protocols using the scheme and achieved 87.5% agreement; one of these coders assessed the remaining protocols.

Table 6 contains a cross-tabulation of children's strategy levels as a function of their age level and social class. Children assigned to the first two levels made either global sweeping gestures or haphazard points over the array as they recited number words. Children assigned to intermediate levels (levels 3, 4, and 5) made a visible attempt to structure a means of including elements once and only once in their counts. Children assigned to the most advanced levels (levels 6 and 7) structured quasi-systematic or systematic strategies to ensure an accurate count. Mann-Whitney U tests revealed that 4-year-olds tended to use more sophisticated strategies than did 2-year-olds (middle class, $z = 4.09$, $p < .0001$; working class, $z = 3.88$, $p < .0001$). We found no effects for social class.

TABLE 5

Strategy Levels Used to Code Children's Unassisted Counting on the Complex Counting Task for Set 13

Level	Description
1	*No strategy.*—The child either refuses to participate or does not produce a discernible strategy (e.g., the child sweeps his or her hand across board with no attempt to indicate particular dots).
2	*Proximal strategy.*—The child may point to as many as five adjacent dots in a sequence.
3	*Primitive mixed strategy.*—The child points to more than five but less than nine adjacent dots on the periphery of the figure as he or she counts in one direction. The child may then stop or continue counting.
4	*Peripheral-only strategy.*—The child points to eight or more peripheral adjacent dots continuing in one direction and then stops.
5	*Peripheral-internal strategy.*—The child points to eight or more peripheral adjacent dots and then counts the dots in middle row without returning to top or bottom rows.
6	*Advanced mixed strategy.*—The child uses one of two types of strategies. *a) Advanced peripheral.*—The child begins with a peripheral strategy but then changes to a linear strategy. *b) Degenerate linear.*—The child uses left-to-right or right-to-left strategy with minor deviations (e.g., counts a row twice or counts first top row, then bottom row, and then middle row).
7	*Linear strategy.*—The child counts either up and down columns, back and forth rows, or each row from left to right or right to left.

Note.—Children were assigned the highest-numbered code if they produced multiple counts.

Number Reproduction Task

We analyzed children's performance on the number reproduction task in two ways. The first analysis concerned whether the child successfully reproduced the model. The second focused on children's strategies.

Accuracy.—For each level of set size, children were assigned a "pass" score if they reproduced the model set accurately and a "fail" score if they

TABLE 6

Percent Distribution of Children's Unassisted Solution Strategies on the Complex Counting Task

	Strategy Level						
Group	1	2	3	4	5	6	7
Middle class:							
2-year-olds[a]	50	20	10	10	5	5	0
4-year-olds[a]	5	20	5	5	15	25	25
Working class:							
2-year-olds[b]	28	50	6	12	6	0	0
4-year-olds[a]	5	10	35	0	5	10	35

[a] $N = 20$.
[b] $N = 18$.

TABLE 7

PERCENTAGE OF CHILDREN ACHIEVING AN ACCURATE SOLUTION ON NUMERICAL
REPRODUCTION TASK AS A FUNCTION OF AGE GROUP, SOCIAL CLASS,
AND TASK CONDITION

Age Group	Middle Class	Working Class
Set 3:		
2-year-olds	15	12
4-year-olds	75	55
Set 9:		
2-year-olds	0	0
4-year-olds	15	5

did not. Table 7 contains the distribution of children's pass/fail scores as a function of age group, social class, and set size. Chi-square analyses revealed that, on set 3, 4-year-olds in both social class groups successfully reproduced the model more frequently than did 2-year-olds (middle class: $\chi^2[1, N = 40$, with Yates correction] $= 12.22, p < .0005$; working class: $\chi^2[1, N = 37$, with Yates correction] $= 7.54, p < .01$). However, on set 9, only three middle-class and one working-class 4-year-old produced an accurate solution, and age differences were not significant because of the small variation in children's successful solutions in either social class group.

Strategies.—It was possible to assign strategy-level codes to children's performance on the large but not on the small set-size condition. Table 8 contains a description of these levels. Interrater agreement on a random sample of 12 set 9 tasks was 92%.

Table 9 contains the cross-tabulation of children's strategy levels as a function of age and SES for set size 9. Children who were assigned to level 1 generally took some or all of the pennies without any attempt to produce a numerical representation of the copy or model. Children assigned to levels 2

TABLE 8

STRATEGY LEVELS USED TO CODE CHILDREN'S UNASSISTED SOLUTIONS ON THE
NUMBER REPRODUCTION TASK FOR SET 9

Level	Description
1	The child either refuses to participate (merely collects pennies in a pile without reference to model set) or produces an inaccurate copy by using some, none, or all of the elements in the available set to constitute a copy. The child shows no visible counting activity during the reproduction.
2	The child produces an inaccurate copy by using some or all of the elements in the available set. The child counts either the model array or the copy, but not both, and does not base modifications of the copy on his or her counting.
3	Same as level 2, but the child counts both the model and the copy.
4	The child counts both the model and the copy; the child uses the products of counting to modify the model, either through trial and error or systematically.

TABLE 9

Percent Distribution of Strategy Levels for Set Size 9 of Numerical
Reproduction Task

	Strategy Level			
Group	1	2	3	4
Middle class:				
2-year-olds[a]	95	0	5	0
4-year-olds[a]	40	15	30	15
Working class:				
2-year-olds[b]	94	0	6	0
4-year-olds[a]	70	15	10	5

[a] $N = 20$.
[b] $N = 18$.

and 3 counted, but their counting was focused on single arrays, and they did
not use their counting to aid their reproduction. Only children assigned to
the highest level used their counting as a means to reproduce the model
accurately, some by trial and error and others systematically. Strategy-level
differences as a function of age group were significant only for the middle-
class children: middle-class 4-year-olds performed at more advanced strategy levels than did the 2-years-olds (Mann-Whitney U test, $z = 3.59$, $p <$
.0005). Strategy-level differences as a function of social class groups were
significant only for the 4-year-olds: middle-class 4-year-olds used higher-
level strategies than did the working-class 4-year-olds (Mann-Whitney U
test, $z = 2.06$, $p < .05$).

SUMMARY AND DISCUSSION

Our results indicate developments across a wide range of numerical
abilities in the 2½–4½-year age period, findings that are very much in accord with recent work on the early development of children's numerical
skills and abilities (Fuson & Hall, 1983; Gelman & Gallistel, 1978; Wagner &
Walters, 1982). There were also some social class differences, particularly in
the tasks involving more complex goal structures. While we found no differences between middle- and working-class children's counting words, their
ability to read numerals, their comparison of number words, or their counting accuracy (tasks involving level 1 and 2 goals), we did find that middle-
class children achieved more advanced performances on tasks involving
cardinality, numerical reproduction, and arithmetic (tasks involving level 3
and 4 goals).

Analyses of age-related shifts in children's strategies on the complex
counting and number reproduction tasks paralleled our analyses of children's shifting goals. The complex counting activity is a level 2 activity: the

child must achieve a numerical representation of a single array of elements. It appeared that many of the younger children in our study transformed this level 2 structure into a level 1 structure: their low accuracy scores were often based either on global correspondences as they recited number words, sweeping their hands across the objects, or on haphazard counting procedures as they assigned number words to objects. For these children, it appeared that the goal of the task was to use number words in the context of some form of nonnumerical referential activity. The older children appeared to structure the activity with respect to the level 2 goals: they tended to produce systematic count strategies, strategies that were adapted with varying degrees of adequacy to the production of cardinal representations.

The numerical reproduction task is a level 3 activity: the child must produce a representation of one array and then produce a numerically equivalent copy of that array. As in the case of the complex counting task, many of the younger children and some of the older ones appeared to transform the goal structure of the task into a lower-level task structure. For instance, the children assigned to the low-strategy categories took some of the pennies without any overt attempt to produce a numerical representation of a single array. Other children attempted to produce representations of one array through counting but did not use the information to produce a numerical equality. Only a few older children counted the model and used that representation as a basis for counting and achieving an accurate copy.

The results of this chapter provide evidence of shifts in the nature of young children's numerical goals over the course of their early development. The 2½-year-olds' numerical problem-solving strategies and achievements as indexed by our tasks provided evidence that they were generating level 1 (e.g., nominal enumeration) or, perhaps, level 2 (cardinal/ordinal representation) goals but not the higher-level goals. In contrast, the 4½-year-olds' performance provided evidence that they were often generating level 3 (comparison/reproduction) and level 4 (arithmetic) goals in addition to the less complex goals.

That children generated numerical goals in our assessment tasks without direct guidance provides an indication that children are involved with independent activity involving number in their everyday lives even as young as 2 years of age. As we have argued, however, this independent goal-directed activity is often set in a social context whose organization depends on the activity of other people. We turn next to our second two components that focus on social processes in children's goal-directed activities involving number—social analyses that provide a basis for understanding how children's self-generated activities may become interwoven with cultural forms of number representation and understanding.

PART 3
SECOND COMPONENT:
THE SOCIAL CONTEXTS
OF CHILDREN'S DEVELOPMENT

INTRODUCTION TO PART 3

A robust association between social class and children's scores on psychometric measures of intelligence has motivated the study of social factors that may affect children's intellectual development (see White, 1982). This "cognitive socialization" literature has shown that children who score higher on measures of intelligence are children reared in homes in which parents have higher aspirations for their children (e.g., Dave, 1963; Kellaghan, 1977; Marjoribanks, 1972, 1977; Mosychuk, 1969; Wolf, 1964) or whose environments are rated higher on indices of "stimulation" on measures of such variables as maternal language (Hess & Shipman, 1965), provision of appropriate play materials (Bradley & Caldwell, 1976; Bradley, Caldwell, & Elardo, 1977), or maternal teaching styles (Bee, Van Egeren, Streissguth, Nyman, & Leckie, 1969; Brophy, 1970). Though the findings of the socialization literature point to social factors as influencing children's intellectual development, these findings do not provide insight into how characteristics of the child (e.g., the child's understanding and goal-directed activities) may play a role in structuring socially organized environments or how other people may contribute to the goals children structure in their everyday play.

In Part 3, we have two concerns. First, as does the prior cognitive socialization literature, we sought to gather information on the values concerning educational achievements held by the parents of the 2½- and 4½-year-olds in our sample (Chap. IV). Such information provides an index of the general orientation of the home setting to children's intellectual activities involving number. Marked differences in values concerning education may be a source of differences in how children's socially organized activities involving number are supported in the home. Second, and of central importance to our treatment, we inquire into the nature of children's numerical activities in the home setting. Our analyses concern the extent to which children generate their own activities as well as the goals entailed in the socially organized activities with which they are engaged. We analyze whether and in what way the goal structures of these numerical activities are related to their numerical understandings as a function of their age level and social class group.

IV. MOTHERS' VALUES AND ASPIRATIONS RELATED TO THEIR CHILDREN'S EDUCATIONAL AND OCCUPATIONAL ACHIEVEMENTS

This chapter contains the results of our assessments of mothers' attitudes and aspirations related to their children's achievement. After a review of available instruments, we found that the one most closely suited to our needs was a scale developed by Marjoribanks (1979) for school-aged populations. We supplemented and adjusted his schedule to assess mothers' attitudes about the value of preschool learning and numerical activities.

METHOD

Procedures

Our interview was designed to elicit three kinds of information: information about each mother's educational aspirations for her child, her occupational aspirations for her child, and her aspirations for her child's competency with basic school-related skills (e.g., telling time, reading, and counting). The interview lasted about 20 min.

Interview

Today, I'd like to ask you some questions about your attitudes toward preschool learning and your hopes for [child's name]'s education and choice of job. If you're unclear about something or want me to repeat something, please feel free to ask. OK?

Questions concerning Educational Aspirations

1. How much education do you hope or wish [child's name] will receive? [the interviewer presented the mother with the following alternatives in both verbal and printed form] (1) elementary school, (2)

junior high school, (3) vocational high school, (4) regular high school, (5) 2-year college or post–high school vocational training, (6) 4-year college, or (7) graduate or professional school.

2. How likely do you really think it is that [child's name] will receive the level of education you hope? Do you think that it's (1) unlikely, (2) likely, or (3) very likely?

3. Since things do not always turn out the way we want them to, how much education do you really expect [child's name] to receive? [The interviewer again presented the mother with the seven alternatives used in question 1.]

Questions concerning Occupational Aspirations

4. What kind of job do you hope [child's name] will have when he/she grows up? [Code: Mean of Duncan ratings for elicited occupation(s).]

5. How likely do you think it is that [child's name] will actually have that job or one as good? Do you think it is (1) very likely, (2) likely, or (3) unlikely?

6. Since children do not always obtain as good a job as parents might hope, what kind of job do you expect [child's name] will have when he/she grows up? [Code: Mean of Duncan ratings for elicited occupation(s).]

7. I'm going to read you a list of occupations, and I'd like you to imagine, for each one, how you would feel if it turned out that it was [child's name]'s permanent occupation when he/she grows up. We know that parents want their children to be happy and that it is hard to think so far into the future, but I'd still like you to try to imagine how you would honestly feel if things worked out so that [child's name]'s occupation were one of the following. Do you think you'd be disappointed or not disappointed? hotel maid or bellhop, dishwasher, nurse's aid/orderly, waiter/waitress, barber/hairdresser, tailor/dressmaker-seamstress, building superintendent, window dresser, telephone operator, bank teller, actor/actress, social worker, computer programmer, high school teacher, author, accountant, reporter, architect, lawyer, or dentist. [These occupations were presented in random order and reflected the full range of the Duncan scale. An index of occupational aspirations was computed by adding the number of items for which mothers reported disappointment. Higher scores thus reflected higher expectations.]

Questions concerning Children's Achievements
during the Preschool Years

8. How important do you think it is that [child's name] know the following things before starting elementary school? [the mother was asked to rate the importance of each item on a seven-point scale from

"not at all important" to "extremely important"] (1) the alphabet, (2) how to write his/her name, (3) how to read (beginning), (4) how to count, (5) how to tell time, and (6) how to do simple addition.

9. I'm going to read you a statement. I'd like you to give me the answer that is closest to what you believe. Remember, there is no right or wrong answer. The best answer you can give is what you believe. Here's another card for you to refer to for the next question. [The card contained a seven-point rating scale from "strongly disagree" to "strongly agree."] "Some children just do not learn much in school. There is nothing that can be done about it."

RESULTS

Table 10 contains the results of our analyses for each of the questions concerned with mothers' educational and occupational aspirations for their children.

TABLE 10

MOTHERS' EDUCATIONAL AND OCCUPATIONAL ASPIRATIONS FOR THEIR CHILDREN AS A
FUNCTION OF SOCIAL CLASS AND CHILDREN'S AGE

| | MIDDLE CLASS | | WORKING CLASS | |
MEASURE	M	SD	M	SD
Educational aspirations:				
1. Educational aspirations (7):				
2-year-olds	6.2	.9	5.6	1.0
4-year-olds	6.2	.7	6.2	.8
2. Likelihood of achievement (3):				
2-year-olds	1.4	.7	1.6	.5
4-year-olds	1.4	.6	1.6	.5
3. Expectation of achievement (7):				
2-year-olds	5.6	1.3	4.5	.9
4-year-olds	6.0	.7	5.4	1.1
Occupational aspirations:				
4. Occupational aspirations (99):				
2-year-olds	75.8	11.8	69.9	19.6
4-year-olds	73.1	15.7	72.0	17.0
5. Likelihood of attainment (3):				
2-year-olds	1.5	.6	1.7	.7
4-year-olds	1.6	.7	1.6	.6
6. Expectation of attainment (99):				
2-year-olds	77.6	9.0	65.4	16.0
4-year-olds	61.5	17.6	55.6	18.0
7. Disappointment scale (20):				
2-year-olds	7.9	2.8	7.8	3.8
4-year-olds	8.2	2.2	7.4	3.0

NOTE.—Numbers in parentheses indicate highest possible score on measure.

Educational Aspirations

Mothers were assigned scores of 1–7 as an index for both their aspirations for their children's achievement and their actual expectations for their children's achievement, and they were assigned scores of 1–3 as an index of their perceptions of the likelihood that their children would accomplish the level of education cited (1 = unlikely, 2 = likely, and 3 = very likely). In general, both population groups had high aspirations for their children, though, when asked what level of education they actually expected their children to achieve, middle-class mothers responded with a significantly higher occupational level than did working-class mothers, $F(1,76) = 14.17$, $p < .001$, and mothers of the 2-year-olds had greater expectations than did mothers of the 4-year-olds, $F(1,76) = 6.71$, $p < .05$.

Occupational Aspirations

The findings in Table 10 on mothers' occupational aspirations for their children are similar to those concerning their educational aspirations. In general, mothers' occupational aspirations for their children are quite high in both social class groups, though, when asked what occupational status they actually expected their children to achieve, the expectations of the middle-class mothers tended to be higher than those of the working-class mothers, $F(1,76) = 3.84$, $p < .10$, and mothers' expectations for the 2-year-olds were higher than mothers' expectations for the 4-year-olds, $F(1,76) = 9.18$, $p < .005$.

Values concerning Preschool Learning

Table 11 contains our analyses of mothers' expressed values concerning the importance of preschool learning. In general, mothers in our sample valued preschool learning, and we found no social class differences on these measures. The only significant age difference we found was that mothers of 2-year-olds thought it was more important for children to tell time prior to school entry than mothers of 4-year-olds did, $F(1,76) = 4.90$, $p < .05$. Virtually all the mothers in our sample responded that they themselves had the ability to influence their children's learning and subsequent academic achievement.

SUMMARY AND DISCUSSION

The findings presented in this chapter indicate that children across our social class and age groups are reared in home contexts that share similar

TABLE 11

MOTHERS' JUDGMENTS ABOUT THE IMPORTANCE OF PRESCHOOL LEARNING IN SELECTED
DOMAINS AS A FUNCTION OF SOCIAL CLASS AND CHILDREN'S AGE

	MIDDLE CLASS		WORKING CLASS	
DOMAIN	M	SD	M	SD
Alphabet (7):				
2-year-olds	6.7	.8	6.7	.7
4-year-olds	6.9	.3	6.3	1.5
Writing (7):				
2-year-olds	6.0	1.3	6.2	1.3
4-year-olds	6.5	.9	6.0	1.5
Reading (7):				
2-year-olds	5.5	1.7	4.8	1.7
4-year-olds	4.9	1.6	5.0	1.9
Counting (7):				
2-year-olds	6.2	1.1	6.3	.9
4-year-olds	6.6	.8	6.3	1.5
Time (7):				
2-year-olds	3.1	1.5	3.8	1.4
4-year-olds	4.3	1.7	4.3	2.0
Addition (7):				
2-year-olds	4.5	1.7	4.4	1.7
4-year-olds	4.8	1.4	4.9	1.6
Ability to influence learning (7):				
2-year-olds	6.2	1.5	6.2	1.4
4-year-olds	6.8	.4	6.3	1.5

NOTE.—Numbers in parentheses indicate highest possible rating.

educational values. Both social class groups had high levels of aspirations for children's achievement. Mothers' responses indicated that they believed that their children would achieve high-status jobs, that their children would achieve high levels of education, and that the mothers themselves would be disappointed if their children did not achieve jobs of a moderate status. Mothers across both social class groups generally placed a high value on their preschoolers' early achievements: mothers believed that it was important, prior to school entry, for their children to gain some mastery of counting, addition, the alphabet, and writing their name. Most mothers strongly believed that they could influence their children's learning.

The social class groups diverged in their responses to questions in which the interviewer pointed out that often children do not achieve what one would hope for. Working-class mothers (perhaps realistically) adjusted their expectations to lower levels of achievement than middle-class mothers did in response to this probe.

On the basis of past research on social class differences in parental aspirations and our findings of differences in children's numerical achievements, we expected to find differences in the educational values and aspirations of mothers across the social class groups. The lack of differences, therefore, is puzzling. We can speculate that one possibility for the high aspirations across groups is due to a self-selection factor: despite our payment incentive to subjects for their participation in the study, our sample may have consisted of mothers particularly interested in the educational achievements of their children. Another possible explanation is that past research that revealed lower aspirations among working-class parents has involved parents of school-aged rather than preschool-aged children; working-class parental aspirations may decline once children enter the school environment and meet with some degree of failure. Regardless, knowledge about maternal values and aspirations regarding education is not a useful predictor of the numerical achievements of children in our sample.

V. THE SOCIAL ORGANIZATION OF NUMBER ACTIVITIES IN THE HOME SETTING

The purpose of the present chapter is to document the number activities with which children are engaged in their homes and age and social class differences in these activities. Mothers' reports of home activities are analyzed for dyads' interest in them, their frequency, and their goal structure complexity. It is our assumption that, through participation in home activities, children acquire numerical competencies. Therefore, results from these analyses will be examined in relation to our previous findings on children's numerical understandings and achievements (from Chap. III).

METHOD

Procedures

To investigate age and social class differences in children's home involvement with number activities, we developed an interview procedure that addressed five categories of number activities. These categories were identified during pilot study and included commercial games specifically designed to teach about number, commercial games that used number but were not specifically designed to teach about number, number games and activities of the mother and child's own invention, commercial books for children containing number activities, and educational television shows containing number activities.

Interview.—The complete interview format is contained in Appendix A. In the interview, the mother was asked to describe number activities (if any) she played with her child in each of our five categories. Following a description of activities in each category, the interviewer recorded the name of each activity on a separate 3 × 5-inch card for later use. For each activity, mothers were questioned about the approximate frequency of play. Mothers were then asked to order the cards in two ways for each category: first, from those activities the child played most often to those the child played least often and, then, from those the mother thought were most important for teaching and learning about number to those she thought were least important. Once the interview was completed for each of the five categories, mothers were presented with all cards irrespective of category. The mother was again asked to order the cards in the same two ways; first, from those the child played most often to those the child played least often and, then, from those the mother thought were most important for teaching and learning about number to those she thought were least important. The measures of frequency of children's participation in number activities were based on maternal ratings of frequency of play within and across activity categories. The measures of goal structure complexity were based on a scheme that corresponded to the four levels of goal complexity presented in Chapter I. (Television shows were excluded because, in these activities, mothers did not play an active role.)

Immediately following the discussion and ratings of home activities, mothers were questioned about mother-child interest in number play. Mothers were asked whether their children ever counted spontaneously and, if so, the frequency of spontaneous counting. Mothers were also asked to rate their children's interest and their own interest in number activities on a seven-point scale (1 = not very interested at all, 7 = extremely interested). All interviews were audiotaped for later coding.

RESULTS

Mothers' and Children's Interest in Number Activities

Table 12 contains a percent distribution of the frequency of children's self-initiated number activities. Nearly the entire sample of mothers reported that children spontaneously engaged in number activities more than once a week, and the large majority reported that they observed their children engaged in self-initiated number activities more than three times a week. Spontaneous activities included counting toys and snacks, reading number books, and using numbers in play (e.g., counting "one, two, three," before jumping off their beds).

Table 13 contains mothers' ratings of their children's interest and their own interest in play with number activities on a seven-point scale (1 = little interest, 7 = extreme interest). Mothers across social class and age groups rated both their children and themselves as having considerable interest in number play. A 2 (age) × 2 (social class) ANOVA on mothers' ratings of children's interest revealed no effects for either social class or age. A 2 (age)

TABLE 12

PERCENT DISTRIBUTION OF CHILDREN'S SELF-INITIATED NUMBER ACTIVITIES

	FREQUENCY OF COUNTING		
GROUP	1	2	3
Middle class:			
2-year-olds[a]	10	20	70
4-year-olds[a]	10	5	85
Working class:			
2-year-olds[b]	0	28	72
4-year-olds[a]	5	25	70

Note.—1 = less than once per week; 2 = once or twice per week; 3 = 3 or more times per week.
[a] $N = 20$.
[b] $N = 18$.

TABLE 13

MOTHERS' AND CHILDREN'S MEAN INTEREST LEVELS IN NUMBER PLAY

	MEAN INTEREST LEVEL	
GROUP	Mothers	Children
Middle class:		
2-year-olds	4.6	4.8
4-year-olds	5.5	5.7
Working class:		
2-year-olds	5.2	5.1
4-year-olds	4.8	5.3

Note.—1 = little interest; 7 = extreme interest.

× 2 (social class) ANOVA on mothers' ratings of their own interest revealed a significant interaction, $F(1,74) = 5.02$, $p < .05$, and no main effects: the mothers of the middle-class 2-year-olds reported less interest than the mothers of the working-class 2-year-olds did, but the mothers of the middle-class 4-year-olds reported more interest than the mothers of the working-class 4-year-olds did. Even so, mothers' ratings are all fairly high, with means ranging from 4.6 to 5.5.

Frequency of Activities

Table 14 contains the percent distribution of mothers who reported play more than once per week for each category of number activity. The entire sample played a number game of their own invention at least once a week, and all but one child in the sample watched an educational television show involving number at least once a week. In addition, the majority of mothers reported play at least once a week for each of the other three categories.

TABLE 14

PERCENTAGE OF MOTHERS REPORTING FREQUENCY OF PLAY GREATER THAN ONCE PER
WEEK FOR SELECTED ACTIVITY TYPES

	ACTIVITY TYPES				
GROUP	Teaching	Using	Own Invention	Books	Television
Middle class:					
2-year-olds	65	50	100	55	100
4-year-olds	70	55	100	75	95
Working class:					
2-year-olds	78	44	100	55	100
4-year-olds	60	55	100	55	100

A 2 (age) × 2 (social class) × 5 (activity type, repeated) ANOVA on mothers' reported frequencies of play revealed a main effect for activity type, $F(4,230) = 41.7, p < .0001$, but no main effects for age or social class and no interactions. Duncan post hoc comparisons ($p < .05$) revealed that games that mothers and children invented and television shows were the most frequent number activities, followed by games designed to teach numbers and, then, number books and games using numbers. Of all the educational television shows, mothers reported that "Sesame Street" was watched most often: all but one mother reported that her child watched "Sesame Street" at least three times per week.

The nature of dyads' number activities in most categories was varied. Reported commercial games designed to teach about numbers included diverse activities, ranging from a number robot (which lit up and rang bells when the sum of the plastic numerals placed on its two arms was equal) to more conventional number activities such as "Sesame Street" flash cards (containing, e.g., a picture of a cone with seven scoops of ice cream on one side and the numeral "7" on the other). Commercial games that used number but were not specifically designed to teach number included games such as dominoes, connect the dots, and Candyland. For games of this type, play required some form of numerical understanding, but achieving this understanding was not the object of the game (the distinction between activities teaching number and activities using number was the mothers'—see App. A). Reports of games of the mothers' and children's own invention included such everyday events as counting steps, figuring out how many plates were required to set the dinner table, and reading numbers on automobile license plates. Reports of number books included books specifically designed to engage children in number activities such as counting, numeral recognition, and the numerical comparison of sets of objects. Reports of television programs included educational shows that typically have a component devoted to teaching number, such as "Sesame Street."

TABLE 15

Examples of Activities at Each of the Four Goal Levels

Level	Description
1	Activities requiring numerical signifiers without numerical operations.
	"One Two Buckle My Shoe" record.—First he listens to the record and tries to sing along. Then, I encourage him to sing it.
	Pushing elevator buttons.—I tell him the button number, and he has to recognize it.
	Magnetic numbers.—I ask him to put the numbers on the refrigerator and watch to see how he puts them. While he puts them, I'm saying number words.
2	Activities entailing numerical representations of single sets.
	Counting coins.—I have a big bowl of coins in the closet. He goes for them but can't pick them up, and he usually tips them over. I encourage him to pick them up and put them in paper cups. I ask him to count as he puts them in. He can go up to 10 sometimes. Occasionally he skips a number; he always picks them up or points.
	Counting fingers and toes.—I say, "Let's see how many you have." He repeats each number with me as we touch his finger, and we count each one. He'll start by himself and go up to three.
	Television channels.—I ask him to put on a particular TV station. If he is to press channel 7, I have him count up to seven. The channel numbers are in a line; channel 7 is bigger than channel 2.
3	Activities entailing numerical comparisons of at least two sets.
	Money equivalences.—I show him that five pennies are the same as a nickel. Sometimes I try dimes and quarters and their relations to the other coins.
	Number cutouts.—I take out any four number cutouts, and I name them and then ask him to name them. I also put the corresponding number of pennies under two cutouts, and I have him count them and say which is more.
4	Activities entailing arithmetic operations.
	Addition with coins.—I put down four pennies here and three pennies there, and he counts each, then counts them altogether up to seven.
	Addition and subtraction with fingers.—I usually use five on one hand and then add with the other hand. Sometimes I do subtraction.
	Addition and subtraction with Chinese checkers.—I put down Chinese checkers, and he counts them. Then, I either add or subtract another one, and he has to tell me how many there are again (up to five marbles).

Goal Structure of Activities

The maternal descriptions of number activities were coded for four levels of goal types on the basis of the analysis of developmental shifts in children's goals (see Chaps. I, III). Table 15 contains the four goal levels and examples of numerical activities at each level. Appendix B contains the complete coding scheme. All interviews were coded by one coder, and 10 randomly selected interviews (including 99 activities) were evaluated by an additional coder. Interrater agreement was 93%.

Goal structure levels.—To generate goal level indices of the most important, the most frequent, and the most complex activities with which dyads were engaged, we used as scores the goal structure complexity codes for the following activities: (1) the activity mothers ranked as most frequent within each category (teaching number, using number, own invention, and number books) and the activity mothers ranked as most frequent irrespective of category (the goal structure of the overall most frequent activity across the activity categories); (2) the activity mothers ranked as most important within each category and the activity mothers ranked as most important irrespective of category; and (3) the most complex activity within each category and the most complex activity irrespective of category, each according to the goal complexity scheme.

The means for the goal level measures of the rankings within category as a function of children's age group and social class are presented in Table 16. Three ANOVAs were performed on these data. Two 2 (age) × 2 (social class) × 3 (activity type, repeated) ANOVAs were performed on the most frequent and the most important goal level scores (these ANOVAs did not include number books as a level of activity type since number books were not ranked by mothers in our interview procedure—see App. A). A 2 (age) × 2 (social class) × 4 (activity type, repeated) ANOVA on the goal level for the most complex activity was performed. The means for the complexity level scores irrespective of categories are presented in Table 17 (overall most frequent, overall most important, and overall most complex). A 2 (age) × 2 (social class) ANOVA was performed on each of these overall scores (one each for overall most frequent, overall most important, and overall most complex). The results of the ANOVAs are discussed below for each factor that yielded significant effects.

Age.—Mothers of 4-year-olds reported activities with more complex goal structures than did mothers of 2-year-olds on the most frequent activity ranked within categories, $F(1,74) = 8.75$, $p < .005$, the most important activity ranked within categories, $F(1,74) = 15.70$, $p < .0005$, the most complex activity ranked within categories, $F(1,74) = 23.81$, $p < .0001$, the overall most important activity ranked irrespective of category, $F(1,69) = 9.73$, $p < .01$, and the overall most complex activity ranked irrespective of category, $F(1,74) = 27.9$, $p < .0001$.

Social class.—Middle-class mothers reported activities with more complex goal structures than did working-class mothers on the most frequent overall activity, $F(1,74) = 5.47$, $p < .05$, the most important overall activity, $F(1,69) = 14.78$, $p < .001$, and the most complex overall activity, $F(1,74) = 4.24$, $p < .05$. There were no social class differences on these measures for activities ranked within categories.

Age × social class interactions.—We found significant age × social class interactions for the activity mothers reported was the most important, ranked both within activity categories, $F(1,74) = 5.10$, $p < .05$, and irrespec-

TABLE 16

Means of Complexity Levels for Most Frequent, Most Important, and Most
Complex Activities as a Function of Social Class and Age

	Middle Class		Working Class	
	M	SD	M	SD
Most frequent:				
Teaching:				
2-year-olds (8, 7)	2.25	.89	2.29	.49
4-year-olds (12, 12)	2.92	.90	2.42	.79
Using:				
2-year-olds (8, 7)	1.87	.64	2.43	.98
4-year-olds (11, 9)	2.45	.69	2.44	.53
Own invention:				
2-year-olds (17, 17)	2.18	.53	2.12	.60
4-year-olds (16, 16)	2.75	1.18	2.00	.52
Most important:				
Teaching:				
2-year-olds (9, 8)	2.22	.83	2.12	.35
4-year-olds (10, 13)	3.20	.92	2.46	.78
Using:				
2-year-olds (7, 7)	1.86	.38	2.57	.53
4-year-olds (12, 9)	2.42	.67	2.44	.53
Own invention:				
2-year-olds (18, 16)	2.22	.43	2.31	.60
4-year-olds (17, 18)	3.18	1.07	2.33	.84
Most complex:				
Teaching:				
2-year-olds (10, 9)	2.20	.79	2.22	.44
4-year-olds (13, 15)	3.15	.99	2.67	.90
Using:				
2-year-olds (8, 8)	2.00	.76	2.62	.74
4-year-olds (14, 9)	2.57	.65	2.44	.53
Own invention:				
2-year-olds (20, 18)	2.65	.75	2.67	.69
4-year-olds (20, 20)	3.40	.88	3.15	.75
Number books:				
2-year-olds (17, 14)	2.06	.43	1.86	.36
4-year-olds (20, 13)	2.45	.83	2.15	.55

Note.—Activities involving writing numerals were not included. Variation in sample size was due to some mothers not reporting activities for these categories. Numbers in parentheses represent sample sizes for middle class and working class, respectively.

tive of activity categories, $F(1,69) = 13.99$, $p < .001$. In each case, the interaction showed that there was a wider gap between the complexity levels that the middle-class mothers reported as most important for their 2- and 4-year-olds than there was between the complexity levels that the working-class mothers reported for their 2- and 4-year-olds.

Activity type.—There were main effects of activity type for the activity ranked as most important, $F(2,93) = 4.36$, $p < .05$, and most complex,

TABLE 17

MEANS OF COMPLEXITY LEVELS FOR OVERALL MOST FREQUENT, OVERALL MOST
IMPORTANT, AND OVERALL MOST COMPLEX ACTIVITIES AS A FUNCTION
OF SOCIAL CLASS AND AGE

	MIDDLE CLASS		WORKING CLASS	
	M	SD	M	SD
Overall most frequent:				
2-year-olds (17, 16)	2.24	.44	2.00	.37
4-year-olds (17, 14)	2.65	1.06	2.07	.47
Overall most important:				
2-year-olds (15, 13)	2.20	.41	2.15	.38
4-year-olds (18, 13)	3.06	1.00	2.08	.28
Overall most complex:				
2-year-olds (20, 18)	2.90	.72	2.61	.70
4-year-olds (20, 20)	3.75	.64	3.40	.68

NOTE.—Numbers in parentheses represent sample sizes for middle class and working class, respectively.

$F(3,158) = 18.80$, $p < .0001$. Duncan post hoc comparisons revealed that, for the measure of most important activity, activities of the mother's and child's own invention tended to be at more complex levels than were activities using number and that activities intended to teach about numbers did not differ significantly from either of the other activity types ($p < .05$). For the most complex activity, activities of the mother's and child's own invention and activities intended to teach about numbers were at more complex goal levels than were activities using number and number books ($p < .05$).

Range of complexity levels.—Children's performances on the numerical tasks described in Chapter III indicated that the 4-year-olds exhibited more sophisticated performances than did the 2-year-olds on tasks at each of the four complexity levels. This finding suggests that, rather than lower-level activities dropping out of dyadic play, children continue to participate in activities at lower goal levels, the higher-level activities supplementing the lower-level activities. To produce a direct index of the range of activity goal levels with which dyads were engaged, the absolute difference between each dyad's highest- and lowest-level activities was computed. A cross-tabulation of this goal range score as a function of age and social class is contained in Table 18. The table reveals that dyads from each age and social class group were typically involved with activities at multiple goal structure levels. A 2 (age) × 2 (social class) ANOVA on the range scores revealed that dyads increased the range of their activity goal structure levels as a function of age, $F(1,73) = 21.60$, $p < .0001$, and that middle-class dyads were engaged with activities that spanned a greater range of goal levels than were working-class dyads, $F(1,73) = 4.77$, $p < .05$.

TABLE 18

PERCENT DISTRIBUTION OF THE DIFFERENCES BETWEEN DYADS' HIGHEST AND LOWEST
GOAL STRUCTURE LEVELS

GROUP	GOAL RANGE SCORE			
	0	1	2	3
Middle class:				
2-year-olds[a]	20	50	25	5
4-year-olds[a]	10	0	65	25
Working class:				
2-year-olds[b]	33	50	17	0
4-year-olds[a]	10	25	60	5

[a] $N = 20$.
[b] $N = 18$.

SUMMARY AND DISCUSSION

The results of the present chapter provide evidence that children's developing competencies described in Chapter III are supported in children's everyday social activities involving number. We found that both the children and the mothers in our sample had marked interest in activities involving number in their everyday play. Mothers reported that their children spontaneously generated number activities, and they rated both their own and their children's interest in number fairly highly. Mothers across both social class groups reported a high incidence of number play—more than once a week for every dyad in the sample and daily for the majority of dyads. According to mothers' reports, the most frequent type of activity with which children were engaged was activities of the dyads' own invention, activities that emerged in everyday social interactions—a finding that points to the everyday character of children's numerical activities.

In general, we found more complex goal structures in the activities of the dyads containing 4-year-olds than in those of the dyads containing 2-year-olds; we also found more complex goal structures in the activities of the middle-class than of the working-class dyads. Further analyses revealed that dyads were engaged with goal structures at multiple levels of complexity, that 4-year-olds were involved with a greater range of complexity levels than were 2-year-olds, and that middle-class dyads were involved with a greater range of complexity levels than were working-class dyads.

The child's engagement with social activities involving number at multiple levels of complexity corresponds to the child's elaboration of forms and functions of multiple levels of complexity reported in Chapter III. It is likely that the multilevel organization of a child's social activities and his or her developing competence support and enrich one another in complex ways. For instance, with progress in formulating numerical reproduction goals in social activities (level 3), the child may generate additional insight about the utility of cardinal number representations (level 2); and, with the intent to represent higher numerical values in play (level 2), the child may generate new insights about the utility of greater number word values (level 1). Conversely, with a child's generation of increasing knowledge of the number word string (level 1), he or she may attempt to identify cardinal/ordinal representation goals that make use of this knowledge in social activities involving number (level 2); similarly, with a child's increasing facility to structure means to represent cardinal values (level 2), he or she may seek to identify additional ways to make use of this capability in the production of numerical comparisons and reproductions in activities like setting the table (level 3). Later, in Chapter VIII, we offer evidence that any single activity may also entail goals at a variety of levels and point to the interplay between children's generation of forms and of functions in single activities over time.

The corresponding age and social class differences in children's achievements (reported in Chap. III) and the overall goal structure of numerical activities with which children are engaged (reported in this chapter) could arise in one of three ways. First, mothers may adjust the complexity of numerical activities to their children's abilities. If this were the case, the correspondence would arise from mothers' knowledge of their children's numerical capabilities and their selection of appropriate activities for their children. Second, children may adjust their own generation of numerical goals and, hence, their numerical accomplishments to their mothers' selection and organization of numerical activities. If this were the case, the correspondence would arise from mothers' selection of activities that they themselves valued and from their children's efforts to accomplish the goals entailed in these activities (to the extent that such accomplishments were within the bounds of the children's capabilities).

The third possible source of the correspondence, and the position that we favor and produce supporting evidence for in Chapters VI–VIII, is an integration of the first and second positions: the correspondence arises from reciprocal adjustments between child and mother. In adult-child interactions—whether these interactions begin in child-initiated spontaneous play or in activities an adult introduces—the participants share in constructing the organization of a number activity: the mothers' task-organizing efforts may be dependent both on their knowledge of their children's competencies at solving number-related problems and on their children's successes and failures to accomplish the goals during the course of an activity. At the same time, children may structure goals in activities that reflect both the understanding they bring to the task and their mothers' efforts at task organization. Thus, in everyday activities, interactions between mother and child may provide conditions that influence the specific numerical goals children form and, thereby, their numerical achievements; in turn, the character of children's achievements may influence the kinds of social activities with which children become engaged. We turn next to analyses of such a negotiation process in mother-child teaching interactions during selected activities.

PART 4
THIRD COMPONENT:
THE EMERGENT ORGANIZATION
OF CHILDREN'S NUMERICAL ACTIVITIES
IN SOCIAL INTERACTIONS

INTRODUCTION TO PART 4

The analysis of mother-child teaching interactions has been an active research concern for the past 3 decades. The focus has been on analyses of maternal directives in these interactions to the neglect of how maternal behaviors interact with children's own goal-directed activities. Here, we review basic elements of past approaches and set our approach in the context of these traditions.

In the 1960s and 1970s, researchers generated information about maternal teaching styles and the way such styles vary as a function of social class (e.g., Bee et al., 1969; Brophy, 1970; Hess & Shipman, 1965). Results indicated that mothers from low social class groups, compared to middle-class mothers, were more directive and punitive, less responsive, less cooperative, less affectionate, more restrictive, and less involved with teaching and playing interactively. More recently, researchers have produced more differentiated analyses that address specific covariates of social class such as mothers' ethnicity and educational level. For instance, Laosa (1980) compared the teaching styles of Chicano and Anglo mothers from a range of social class levels as they attempted to teach their kindergarten children to solve Tinkertoy puzzles. Chicano mothers tended to be more directive, offer less praise, and more frequently model the solution of problems than Anglo mothers. However, when the mothers' educational level was used as a covariate, all effects for ethnic background disappeared.

In the 1970s and 1980s, a number of studies have been published inspired by Vygotsky's (1962, 1978; cf. Wertsch, 1986) writings on the "zone of proximal development" (e.g., Rogoff, Ellis, & Gardner, 1984; Rogoff & Gardner, 1981; Saxe, Gearhart, & Guberman, 1984; Wertsch, 1979, 1984; Wood, Bruner, & Ross, 1976; Wood & Middleton, 1975). Unlike the socialization tradition, Vygotsky argued that a developmental approach to understanding the social roots of intelligence should consist of assessments of both the child's performance in solving a problem alone and the child's accomplishments when assisted by adults or more capable peers. From Vygotsky's perspective, the "zone" between the child's unassisted performance and what the child can accomplish with assistance provides the effective learning environment for the child's further development as well as the way social and historical achievements of the child's social group (like a number system) become interwoven with the problem-solving activities of the child.

The Vygotsky-inspired research differs in at least two ways from the studies cited above on the social determinants of children's intellectual development. First, virtually all the Vygotsky-inspired studies have been limited to middle-class populations since the focus has been on intrinsic properties of the interactions rather than on associations between extrinsic variables (e.g., parental aspirations and home stimulation) and children's achievement. Second, there has been a focus on the joint production or "negotiation" of children's environments in teaching interactions. In general, some index of children's competence (e.g., age and successes and failures during the task) has been related to the specificity of adults' directives to children in adult-child tutorial interactions.

Within this tradition, Wood and his collaborators have produced results indicating that effective teaching is typically more directive with younger and/or less able children (Wood et al., 1976; Wood & Harris, 1977; Wood & Middleton, 1975; Wood, Wood, & Middleton, 1978). For example, in one study on tutoring that used age as an index of ability, a tutor's behavior was analyzed as she taught a block-building puzzle task to 3-, 4-, and 5-year-olds (Wood et al., 1976). The tutor's behavior varied markedly with her students' age; the tutor structured the task to a greater extent for the younger children, providing more help and intervening more frequently. Wood and Middleton (1975), defining "ability" as success or failure during the task (tasks with recurring subparts), reported contingent analyses of adults' behavior in relation to children's performance throughout the interactions. They found that mothers who used contingent approaches (i.e., providing more direct assistance after children's errors and less when children succeeded) were more likely to have children who perform effectively when tested on the same task after instruction terminated. In a follow-up study, Wood et al. (1978) assessed the effectiveness of the teaching strategies observed in the previous study using an experimental paradigm. As expected, contingent teaching was more effective than noncontingent teaching.

Wertsch (1979, 1985; Wertsch, McNamee, McLane, & Budwig, 1980), following Vygotsky directly, has argued that higher cognitive functions are rooted in interpsychological functioning. With development, social interchanges are progressively internalized in such a way that the child's problem-solving behaviors, which are initially regulated by an adult or a more capable peer in social interactions, come to be under the control of the child. Wertsch, through an analysis of mother-child teaching interactions involving a truck jigsaw puzzle, identified a sequence of levels of dyadic interaction that reflect the progression from inter- to intrapsychological functioning or other to self-regulation.

The body of research on interactional analyses of children's performances with adult assistance goes further than earlier work in providing an understanding of the social organization of children's experiences. The use of children's age as a variable has shown that adults tailor the nature of their assistance to children's abilities. Contingent analyses of shifts during the interaction in adults' instruction as a function of children's ability to do the task reveal aspects of how children and mothers are jointly constructing children's environments during problem-solving activities. However, a problem with the Vygotsky-inspired work is that no study is guided by a model of the child's developing understandings. Typically, analyses are based solely on functional definitions of cognition: the variables of age and the child's successes and failures during the task are used as indices of some unspecified knowledge state of the child. Where researchers have attempted to characterize young children's understandings, it is with reference to the absence of understanding or to children's lack of comprehension. What is missing in these research programs is a positive analysis of the goals that children are structuring in problem-solving tasks and the relation between these goals and adults' organizing activities—a treatment that can be used to understand the significance of the adult's activities from the perspective of the child.

Lacking in virtually all interactional studies, whether from the Vygotskiian or the socialization traditions, are analyses of sociocultural activities with which children are engaged, analyses in which targeted "laboratory" activities can be situated. Typically, single activities are selected that, at best, are assumed to be representative of some unanalyzed knowledge domain of children's functioning.

The next two chapters contain our analyses of videotaped observations of mother-child interactions during play with number activities. Unlike previous approaches, our analyses are grounded in a general treatment of form-function shifts in children's numerical understandings (Chaps. I, III) and in a sociocultural treatment of the organization of children's numerical activities (Chap. V). The coordination of these two components permits us to interpret how ongoing developmental processes in the child both contribute to and are influenced by the goal structure of socially organized numerical activities. We show how an adult (the mother) may adjust the goal structure of a sociocultural activity to her child's ability to structure numerical goals (and to deploy forms to achieve these goals). In turn, we analyze how the child may adjust his or her numerical goals to that required to accomplish the numerical goals that emerge in an interaction.

For our studies, we used two standard activities that were within the range of activity levels with which our dyads were engaged at home and that differed in goal structure complexity—a single-array counting activity (level 2) and a number reproduction activity (level 3). We asked our dyads to play each of these activities at two levels of set size. Varying goal structure complexity and set size (task difficulty) allowed us to observe a range of ways in which mothers adjust activities to mesh with their children's ability to generate numerical goals. Analyses of the observed interactions are reported in Chapter VI for the single-array counting activity and in Chapter VII for the number reproduction activity. In each case, our concern is to understand the joint construction of children's numerical environments during the interactions as a function of children's developing numerical abilities (as indexed by their age level and unassisted performances on the same tasks) and their social class.[4]

[4] Mothers assisted their children with the counting and the number reproduction activities after the children attempted these tasks without assistance (Chap. III). As we report in Chaps. VI and VII, children performed the counting and reproduction tasks far more successfully when assisted by their mothers than when unassisted, a pattern of findings that may reflect some effects of practice. Nevertheless, any effects of practice would have to be modest, at best. We provided no instruction regarding strategy or feedback regarding accuracy in either unassisted task. The changes in children's use of systematic strategies and in their success when assisted by their mothers were quite dramatic, and it is highly doubtful that an unassisted practice session could lead to such qualitative shifts in performance.

VI. THE EMERGENT ORGANIZATION OF NUMERICAL ACTIVITIES IN SOCIAL INTERACTIONS: ANALYSES OF A SINGLE-ARRAY ACTIVITY

In Chapter III, we reported children's unassisted performances on the complex counting task (a level 2 activity) for two set-size conditions, five and 13 elements. Our analyses indicated that the younger children often defined the activity as nonnumerical referential (level 1). The younger children rarely assigned exactly one number word to each and every object; they often produced global correspondences, sweeping their hands across the arrays as they recited number words, or haphazardly assigned number words to objects. In contrast, 4-year-olds tended to structure the activity as the numerical representation of a single array (level 2): they were more likely to use counting strategies that aided their accuracy, although their strategies were frequently not the most effective (linear). The purpose of the present chapter is to understand how children's task solutions are altered as they attempt the complex counting task with their mothers.

METHOD

Procedures

Instructions to mothers.—We gave the mother two boards containing arrays of five and 13 dots and the following instructions:

> I would like you to treat this as an occasion to teach your child about counting as you might do it in everyday activities. There are two boards. I would like you to show this board [set size 5 or 13 in counterbalanced order] to your child first. The object of the game is simply to find the number of dots on the board. Once you finish the first board you can go on to the second one. Remember, what we are really interested in is how you encourage learning and understanding in your child.

Coding

Task analysis.—In the complex counting activity, the goal is to determine the number of dots on the board. In order to achieve this goal, two subgoals must be coordinated and accomplished. One is a correct recitation of the number word sequence, and the other is the assignment of those number words in one-to-one correspondence with target objects.

Organization of coding schemes.—To analyze reciprocal mother-child adjustments during the complex counting activity, we developed two types of schemes, one for mothers' presentations and adjustments of the complex counting tasks to their children's efforts and the other for children's adjustments of their own goal-directed behavior to their mothers' efforts to frame and provide assistance during the task. Each set of schemes is used to document how one participant (the mother or the child) generates or modifies the task context for the other.

1. *Codes for maternal instruction.*—Three schemes were used to code maternal counting assistance, two for maternal instruction with children's correspondence subgoals and the third for maternal instruction with children's number word sequence subgoals.

a) Codes for maternal correspondence instruction.—Tables 19 and 20 contain the schemes for coding maternal correspondence instruction for sets 5 and 13, respectively. Each scheme consists of an ordered set of levels, ranging from maternal directives that indicate the superordinate goal of the task (e.g., instructions to determine the total number of dots) to more specific subgoals (e.g., instructions to count a particular dot). Thus, for both schemes, lower-numbered levels represent mothers' presentation of the superordinate single-array goal of the task, intermediate levels represent mothers' instruction focused on more limited correspondence goals, and the highest levels represent the completion of the goal by the mother. The schemes in Tables 19 and 20 differ in that, for the large-set-size condition (set 13), the use of a counting strategy to keep track of the counted and the yet-to-be-counted objects is critical for accuracy while, for the small-set-size condition (set 5), the dots are few enough in number to keep in mind which has and which has not been counted without a systematic strategy. As a result, only the scheme for set 13 includes codes to document how mothers assist their children in generating an efficient counting strategy.[5]

[5] We included instruction in using a linear strategy as an essential component of maternal correspondence instruction, set 13 (Table 20), on the basis of three considerations. First, Shannon (1978) found that the linear strategy represented the end point of a developmental sequence of children's strategies on this task. Second, a preliminary analysis of the videotapes showed that mothers very rarely encouraged or accepted a count that used a strategy other than a linear one. Third, the analysis of children's unassisted performance revealed that a linear strategy was associated with the lowest incidence of errors.

TABLE 19

A Hierarchical Ordering of Maternal Instructions Related to the
Correspondence Goals of the Task—Maternal Correspondence Scheme: Set 5

Maternal Instruction Level	Example
Instructions pertaining to achieving correspondences with all or several dots:	
0. Mother provides single-array goal of the task or instructs child to count a subset of dots	"Count the dots." "Count the top row of dots."
Instructions pertaining to achieving local correspondences:	
1. Mother instructs child to count a particular dot	"This dot is next."
2. Mother performs correspondence for the child	Mother points while child recites numbers.

TABLE 20

A Hierarchical Ordering of Maternal Instructions Related to the
Correspondence Goals of the Task—Maternal Correspondence Scheme: Set 13

Maternal Instruction Level	Example
Instructions pertaining to the single-array goal of the task:	
0. Mother provides single-array goal but no strategy instruction	"Count the dots."
1. Mother provides single-array goal and general strategy	"Count the dots in rows."
2. Mother provides single-array goal and specific strategy	"First count the top row, then the middle row, and then the bottom row."
Instructions pertaining to achieving local correspondences:	
3. Mother indicates subset of dots to be counted	"Now count this row."
4. Mother instructs child to count a particular dot	"This dot is next."
5. Mother performs correspondence for child	Mother points while child recites numbers.

b) Codes for maternal number word sequence instruction.—Table 21 contains the codes for maternal instruction related to the child's number word sequence subgoals. This scheme contains five ordered levels, ranging from

(The Pearson correlation between strategy-level use and number of gesture errors in the large-set-size condition reported in Chap. III was − .71.)

TABLE 21

A HIERARCHICAL ORDERING OF MATERNAL INSTRUCTIONS RELATED TO THE SEQUENCE
GOALS OF THE TASK—MATERNAL SEQUENCE SCHEME: SETS 5 AND 13

Maternal Instruction Level	Example
0. No sequence-related instruction (in an introduction only)	. . .
1. Mother requests next number without reference to other numbers	"What number is this?"
2. Mother requests next number referring to last number	"What comes after five?"
3. Mother provides a sequence of numbers up to last one recited	"Two, three, four, and then?"
4. Mother provides hints about next number	"T . . . Tw . . . Twel . . ." "How old are you?"
5. Mother provides number	"After six comes seven."

simple requests that the child continue counting to increasing assistance in determining the next number word. Thus, if a child counts, "One, two, three," and then pauses, maternal responses might include, "What comes next?" (level 1), repeating the prior count (level 3), or providing the number for the child (level 5).

c) *Codes for children's counting behaviors as contexts for maternal instruction.*—In order to examine contingent relations between mothers' instructions in organizing the task and children's ongoing task activity, we coded children's counting behaviors between each maternal instruction for the adequacy of their correspondence and sequence performance. Children's correspondence errors included, on either set, skipping a dot and applying more than one distinct number word to the same dot and, on the large set, any deviation from a linear strategy. Children's sequence errors included, on either set, any deviation from the conventional sequence of number words (e.g., starting with a number other than one and counting out of sequence) and pauses in the child's recitation of number words followed by maternal instruction relevant to the number word sequence.

2. *Codes for children's adjustments to maternal instruction.*—We coded children's adjustments to specific types of maternal correspondence instruction and sequence instruction.

a) *Codes for children's adjustments to maternal correspondence instruction.*—Table 22 contains our codes for children's adjustments to three categories of maternal correspondence instruction: general correspondence instruction (maternal requests for the child to count the array), maternal strategy instruction (maternal instruction in using a linear strategy to count the array or a subset of dots), and local correspondence instruction (maternal directives to count a single dot or to point to the dots with her). Criteria were established for the appropriateness of children's responses to each type of maternal instruction. Appropriate adjustments included modifications of children's behavior in accord with the maternal instruction (e.g., a child begins to point to dots following a maternal request to count the array). Partial adjustments included children's responses that were initially in accord with the maternal instruction but did not follow the instruction to completion (e.g., a child counts only two rows on set 13 after maternal instruction to count all the rows). Inappropriate adjustments included responses that demonstrated either incorrect or no modification of behavior in accord with the maternal instruction (e.g., a child points to an already-counted dot following the question, "Which dot is next?").

b) *Codes for children's adjustments to maternal sequence instruction.*—Table 23 contains our codes for children's adjustments to two categories of maternal sequence instruction: general sequence instruction (maternal requests that the child count the array) and local sequence instruction (maternal requests for the first or next in a sequence of number words). In a manner similar to the coding of children's adjustments to maternal correspondence instruction, children's responses to each type of maternal sequence instruction were coded as either appropriate, partial, or inappropriate.

Intercoder agreements.—One of us coded 100% of the videotapes, and a second rater independently coded a random sample of 20% of the videotapes distributed across age and social class groups. Each rater's codes were reduced to the measures used in our analyses (described below in relevant sections of the results), and interrater agreement was computed on the basis of these scores. Agreements for each measure are presented in subsequent sections.

Indices of Children's Unassisted Performance

In order to understand how children's conceptualizations of the task goals both contribute to and are influenced by the goal structure that emerges in dyadic interactions, we derived three indices of children's goals on the basis of their unassisted performances. One measure indexes sequence ability (i.e., recitation of number words) and two measures index correspondence ability (i.e., counting each dot once and only once). Table 24 contains a description of the three measures and their derivation from children's assessments reported in Chapter III.

We derived three levels of children's sequence ability from their achievement in the counting words task: a low-performance group of children who were likely to have difficulty achieving the sequence goals of both set 5 and set 13 during the interactions; a middle-performance group whose counting score indicated sufficient sequence ability only for the small set size; and a high-performance group whose rote-counting score indicated

TABLE 22

Maternal Instruction	Child Adjustment
General correspondence instruction:	
1. "How many dots are there?"	*Appropriate adjustment:* 1a. Child gives a numerical judgment or begins pointing. *Inappropriate adjustment:* 1b. Child does not give numerical judgment or begin pointing.
2. "Count the dots."	*Appropriate adjustment:* 2a. Child begins pointing to dots. *Inappropriate adjustment:* 2b. Child does no pointing.
Maternal strategy instruction: Assistance in using a linear strategy:[a]	
3. "Count the dots in rows."	*Appropriate adjustment:* 3a. Child counts in rows (may skip a dot at beginning or middle of a row). *Partial adjustment:* 3b. Child counts one but not all rows. 3c. Child counts at least one row, interrupted before counting all rows and before erring. *Inappropriate adjustment:* 3d. Child does not complete counting one row. 3e. Child ignores directive.
4. Mother indicates a subset of dots to be counted or the beginning of a row	*Appropriate adjustment:* 4a. Child counts indicated dots (may skip one). *Partial adjustment:* 4b. Child begins counting indicated dots, errs. *Inappropriate adjustment:* 4c. Child counts, but not indicated dots. 4d. Child ignores directive.
5. Mother asks child which is the next row to be counted	*Appropriate adjustment:* 5a. Child correctly counts next row. *Partial adjustment:* 5b. Child begins to count next row, errs. 5c. Child begins to count next row, is interrupted before erring or completing count. *Inappropriate adjustment:* 5d. Child counts, but not the correct row. 5e. Child ignores directive.

TABLE 22 (*Continued*)

Maternal Instruction	Child Adjustment
Local correspondence instruction: Assistance in counting a single dot and joint counts: 6. Mother indicates a dot to be counted at start of a count	*Appropriate adjustment:* 6a. Child counts indicated dot, continues. 6b. Child counts indicated dot, stops. *Inappropriate adjustment:* 6c. Child counts, but not indicated dot. 6d. Child ignores directive.
7. Mother indicates (or asks) which is next dot to count	*Appropriate adjustment:* 7a. Child counts indicated dot. *Inappropriate adjustment:* 7b. Child counts other dot. 7c. Child ignores directive.
8. Mother asks child to point with her or takes child's hand and points	*Appropriate adjustment:* 8a. Child points with mother until end or until mother stops pointing. *Partial adjustment:* 8b. Child points with mother to some dots. *Inappropriate adjustment:* 8c. Child ignores request.

[a] Maternal strategy instruction codes were applied to set 13 only; few mothers used this form of instruction on set 5.

sufficient sequence ability for both sets. The first index of correspondence ability—gesture—is based on children's success in forming one-to-one correspondences in their unassisted performances on the complex counting task. There are three levels: children whose unassisted performances indicated the ability to meet the correspondence goals of neither set, of set 5 but not set 13, and of both sets. The second index of correspondence ability—strategy—is a measure of the counting strategy children used in their unassisted performances in set 13. Three levels were created by collapsing selected strategy types reported in Chapter III: low, indicating no goal to count each and every dot; middle, indicating the goal of counting each dot once and only once but an inadequate strategy for achieving an accurate numerical representation of the array; and high, indicating both the goal of counting each dot once and only once and a strategy well suited to achieving an accurate count.

These measures of unassisted performance were highly related to age

TABLE 23

CODING SCHEME FOR CHILDREN'S ADJUSTMENTS TO MATERNAL
SEQUENCE INSTRUCTION

Maternal Instruction	Child Adjustment
General sequence instruction:	
1. "How many dots are there?"	*Appropriate adjustment:* 1a. Child gives numerical judgment or recites number words. *Inappropriate adjustment:* 1b. Child does not give numerical judgment or recite number words.
2. "Count the dots."	*Appropriate adjustment:* 2a. Child recites number words. *Inappropriate adjustment:* 2b. Child does not recite number words.
Local sequence instruction: Assistance in determining the first or next in a sequence of number words:	
3. Mother asks for first or next word in number word sequence	*Appropriate adjustment:* 3a. Child states correct number. *Partial adjustment:* 3b. Child gives incorrect number. *Inappropriate adjustment:* 3c. Child gives inappropriate response (e.g., "It's a dot"). 3d. No response, ignores request.

TABLE 24

MEASURES OF CHILDREN'S UNASSISTED PERFORMANCES

Measure: Derivation	Level	Description
Sequence: Counting words task	1	Counts to less than five.
	2	Counts to five or more but less than 13.
	3	Counts to 13 or more.
Gesture: Complex counting task (success = number of gestures differs no more than one from number of dots in array)	1	Success on neither set.
	2	Success on one set only.
	3	Success on both sets.
Strategy: Complex counting task (set 13 strategy level)	1	Strategy levels 1–2 (no strategy or proximal strategy).
	2	Strategy levels 3–5 (peripheral strategy).
	3	Strategy levels 6–7 (linear strategy).

NOTE.—Level 1 is low, 2 middle, and 3 high.

but not to social class, a result similar to the analysis of children's abilities on tasks involving level 1 and 2 goals (see Chap. III). (Pearson correlation coefficients of sequence, gesture, and strategy measures with age were .68, .70, and .67, respectively, and with social class were −.01, −.13, and .01, respectively.)

RESULTS

Our analyses consist of two complementary components: (1) analyses of mothers' adjustments to their children's abilities to accomplish the correspondence and sequence subgoals of the task and (2) analyses of children's adjustments to maternal efforts as mothers assisted their children in the task.

Analyses of Maternal Adjustments to Children's Performances

To examine mothers' adjustments to their children's abilities, we analyzed (a) whether mothers matched their type of instruction (i.e., correspondence or sequence instruction) to the subgoal with which their children were experiencing difficulty, (b) whether mothers adjusted the specificity of their instruction as a function of children's ability (using the measures of correspondence and sequence ability derived from children's unassisted performances), and (c) whether mothers offered more specified correspondence and sequence instruction during the interaction in response to children's errors. Examination of social class differences was included in each of these sets of analyses.

To facilitate explanation of the analyses below, we will refer to the following prototypical example to illustrate the measures. In this example, a mother is instructing her child on the set size 13 condition.

1. MOTHER. Count the dots.
2. *Child recites "one" through "six" correctly while haphazardly pointing to dots.*
3. MOTHER. Start over, and this time count the dots in rows.
4. *Child correctly counts the bottom row and continues to count "five, six, eight," while pointing to the first, second, and third dots in the second row.*
5. MOTHER. No. What comes after six?
6. CHILD. 11.
7. MOTHER. Seven comes after six.
8. *Child repeats "seven," counts "eight" and "nine" while pointing to the next two dots, and then begins to point to the first dot of the bottom row again.*
9. MOTHER. You already counted that row. Now count the dots in the top row [pointing to the top row].
10. *Child correctly counts the top row to 13.*

Maternal Instruction by Error Type

The analysis of the match between mothers' instruction type and children's error type (just a correspondence error, just a sequence error, or both kinds of errors) is illustrated in the above example by noting that the child made two correspondence errors (lines 2, 8) and that, after each error, the mother provided just correspondence instruction: "Count the dots in rows" (line 3), and, "Now count the dots in the top row" (line 9). Following each of the child's two sequence errors (lines 4, 6), the mother provided just sequence instruction: "What comes after six?" (line 5), and, "Seven comes after six" (line 7). Thus, in the example, the mother's instruction type always matched the child's error type.

Interrater agreement for coding maternal instruction type following children's errors was computed in two steps. First, agreement for children's errors was 82.2%. Then, for those instances in which the coders agreed on the existence and type of error, agreement for the type of maternal instruction that followed was 96.7%.

Table 25 contains the mean proportion of each type of maternal instruction as a function of children's error types. There was a significant effect for the type of instruction mothers provided in each of our analyses except after children made both correspondence and sequence errors on set 13 (set 5: correspondence errors, $F[2,30] = 9.98, p < .001$; sequence errors, $F[2,34] = 10.69, p < .001$; both errors, $F[2,36] = 8.36, p < .001$; set 13: correspondence errors, $F[2,94] = 21.00, p < .0001$; sequence errors, $F[2,74] = 18.89, p < .0001$). Post hoc Duncan's multiple range tests revealed that all mothers tended to respond to their children's errors with instruction that matched the subgoal with which their children had experienced difficulty: after children made just correspondence errors, mothers were most likely to

TABLE 25

MEAN PROPORTIONS OF TYPES OF MATERNAL INSTRUCTION FOLLOWING
CHILDREN'S ERRORS

	MOTHER'S INSTRUCTION TYPE		
CHILD ERROR	Correspondence	Both	Sequence
Set 5:			
Correspondence (16)	.61	**.24**	**.00**
Sequence (18)	**.09**	**.20**	.63
Both (19)	**.31**	**.54**	.00
Set 13:			
Correspondence (48)	.50	.23	.02
Sequence (38)	**.16**	**.14**	.66
Both (33)	**.38**	**.37**	**.16**

NOTE.—Proportions do not total 100 because some errors were followed by no instruction. Numbers in parentheses represent sample sizes. Adjacent values in boldface type do not differ significantly.

respond with just correspondence instruction, and, following just sequence errors, mothers tended to respond with just sequence instruction. When children made both errors at once, many mothers responded with both types of instruction, although some mothers focused on just correspondence or just sequence instruction.

Appropriate maternal adjustments (instruction that matched the kind of error the child had made—whether alone or combined with other instruction) were examined as a function of age and social class in a set of three 2 (age) × 2 (social class) ANOVAs for each set-size condition. One ANOVA analyzed the kind of instruction mothers provided following children's correspondence-only errors, one was used to analyze differences following children's sequence-only errors, and one was used to analyze differences following simultaneous correspondence and sequence errors. The ANOVAs revealed no age or social class differences in maternal adjustments to their children's errors.

The Specificity of Maternal Instruction

To examine the complexity of the goals mothers specified in their instruction as functions of task complexity, children's abilities, and social class, three measures of the specificity of mothers' instructions were generated. (1) Initial instruction was the mother's first task-relevant instruction and represents the mother's initial formulation of the task for her child. In the above example, the mother's initial instruction is, "Count the dots" (line 1— maternal correspondence scheme: level 0; maternal sequence scheme: level 0). The second two measures are indices of mothers' instructional specificity over the entire interaction (the initial instruction and the remainder of the task); since the interactions of dyads that did not complete the task were often abbreviated, analyses based on these measures exclude dyads that did not complete the entire task successfully.[6] (2) Most specified instruction was

[6] Task success was defined as the accurate determination of the number of dots in the array. The number of dyads who did not successfully complete the task, for sets 5 and 13, respectively, are five and nine middle-class 2-year-olds, zero and two middle-class 4-year-olds, four and nine working-class 2-year-olds, and two and four working-class 4-year-olds. Pearson correlations revealed that older and more able children were more likely to succeed on the task in mother-child interactions (correlations of task success with children's age group and measures of ability range from 0.23 to 0.35, all p's < .05). There was no relation of social class and task success (correlations for sets 5 and 13, respectively, are 0.05 to 0.08, p's = N.S.). Since successful task completion varied across age groups, mothers' most specified instruction and median level of instruction were analyzed two ways—first including only those dyads that did succeed and then including all dyads (i.e., including information from the abbreviated interactions of unsuccessful dyads). The patterns of results of these analyses were the same; therefore, we present results only for those analyses that included only the dyads that successfully completed the task.

71

the highest level of instruction mothers provided at any point in the interaction. In the above illustration, the mother's most specified correspondence instruction is, "Now count the dots in the top row" (line 9—maternal correspondence scheme: level 3), and her most specified sequence instruction is, "Seven comes after six" (line 7—maternal sequence scheme: level 5). (3) Median level of instruction was the median level of all maternal instructions throughout the interaction. In the above example, the mother's median level for correspondence instruction is 1.0 (levels 0, 1, and 4 for lines 1, 3, and 9, respectively); and the mother's median level for sequence instruction is 3.5 (levels 2 and 5 for lines 5 and 7, respectively).

Interrater agreement was computed in terms of Pearson correlations. Correlations between the two coders for sets 5 and 13 were .89 and .76 for initial instruction, 1.00 and .98 for most specified instruction, and .98 and .88 for median level of instruction, respectively.

The relation of task complexity to the specificity of maternal instruction.—Table 26 contains the percentage of mothers who provided more specified instruction on set 5 than on set 13, more specified instruction on set 13 than on set 5, and the same level of instruction on both sets. Sign tests revealed no difference in the specificity of mothers' initial instruction on sets 5 and 13 for either correspondence or sequence goals. Sign tests, however, did reveal significant effects for mothers' most specified instruction (binomial, $N = 23$, $p < .001$, for correspondence instruction; $N = 17$, $p < .001$, for sequence instruction) and median level of instruction (binomial, $N = 35$, $p < .001$, for correspondence instruction; $N = 25$, $p < .05$, for sequence instruction). These findings indicate that, over the course of the interactions but not in their introductions to the task, mothers tended to assist their children on the larger, more difficult set by using more specified instructions and structuring less complex goals.

The relation of children's ability and social class to the specificity of maternal

TABLE 26

Percentage of Mothers Who Provided More, Less, or Equal Levels of Instruction on Set 5 Compared with Set 13

Measure	Correspondence Instruction			Sequence Instruction		
	5 > 13	13 > 5	5 = 13	5 > 13	13 > 5	5 = 13
Initial instruction (70)	9	16	76	4	7	89
Most specified (52)	6	60	35	2	31	67
Median level (52)	10	58	33	12	37	52

Note.—Maternal correspondence instruction on set 13 was recoded using the maternal correspondence scheme for set 5 to allow comparisons across conditions. Numbers in parentheses represent sample sizes.

TABLE 27

PEARSON CORRELATION COEFFICIENTS FOR THREE MEASURES OF MATERNAL
CORRESPONDENCE INSTRUCTION WITH CHILDREN'S UNASSISTED PERFORMANCE, AGE, AND
SOCIAL CLASS FOR SETS 5 AND 13

Maternal Instruction	Unassisted Performance[a]	Age	SES[b]	SES. Unassisted Performance, Age[c]
Set 5:				
Initial instruction				
(74)	−.34**	−.28**	−.12	−.17
Most specified				
(66)	−.69***	−.72***	−.06	−.13
Median level				
(66)	−.64***	−.63***	−.07	−.14
Set 13:				
Initial instruction				
(70)	−.20*	−.32**	−.11	−.14
Most specified				
(53)	−.35**	−.46***	−.40**	−.44***
Median level				
(53)	−.34**	−.57***	−.23*	−.29*

NOTE.—Numbers in parentheses represent sample sizes.

[a] The index of children's unassisted performance for set 5 was the score for gestural accuracy on the unassisted version of the complex counting task; the index for set 13 was the score for counting strategy on the unassisted version of the complex counting task.

[b] 1 = working class; 2 = middle class.

[c] The correlation between measures of maternal correspondence instruction and social class, controlling for unassisted performance and age group.

* $p < .05$.
** $p < .01$.
*** $p < .001$.

instruction.—Table 27 contains Pearson correlation coefficients of the measures of maternal correspondence instruction on sets 5 and 13 with children's age, unassisted performance (gestures for set 5 and strategy for set 13), and social class. For both sets, measures of children's ability were significantly related to the specificity with which mothers presented the correspondence goals of the task. Mothers of older children and mothers of children who were more accurate in creating correspondences in their unassisted performances tended to formulate more complex correspondence goals in their initial instruction, their most specified instruction, and their median level of instruction.

Social class was significantly related to mothers' most specified instruction and median level of instruction on set 13 and remained so when the variance due to children's age and unassisted performance was partialed out; middle-class mothers tended to structure more complex correspondence goals than did working-class mothers on the more difficult condition.

Table 28 contains the Pearson correlation coefficients of measures of maternal sequence instruction with children's age, unassisted performance (sequence), and social class. Both measures of children's ability were

TABLE 28

Pearson Correlation Coefficients for Three Measures of Maternal Sequence Instruction with Children's Unassisted Performance, Age, and Social Class for Sets 5 and 13

Maternal Instruction	Unassisted Performance[a]	Age	SES[b]	SES. Unassisted Performance, Age[c]
Set 5:				
Initial instruction				
(75)	−.31**	−.21*	−.11	−.11
Most specified				
(67)	−.69***	−.68***	.02	.06
Median level				
(67)	−.68***	−.63***	−.04	−.04
Set 13:				
Initial instruction				
(71)	−.30**	−.27*	−.02	−.05
Most specified				
(54)	−.63***	−.42***	−.07	.02
Median level				
(54)	−.57***	−.41***	−.20	−.15

Note.—Numbers in parentheses represent sample sizes.
[a] The index for children's unassisted performance was the score on the unassisted counting words task.
[b] 1 = working class; 2 = middle class.
[c] The correlation between measures of maternal sequence instruction and social class, controlling for unassisted performance and age group.
* $p < .05$.
** $p < .01$.
*** $p < .001$.

significantly related to the specificity of maternal instruction in both sets, except for the relation of age to mothers' initial instruction in set 5—in which most mothers provided no sequence instruction. Mothers of older children and mothers of children who demonstrated greater knowledge of the number sequence in their unassisted performances provided less specified sequence instruction than did mothers of less capable children, a result similar to our findings for maternal correspondence instruction. There were no significant correlations between maternal sequence instruction and social class, a result unlike that for maternal correspondence instruction.

Shifts in the specificity of maternal instruction following children's errors.—To analyze shifts in the specificity of mothers' instruction following correspondence errors, we computed the mean proportion of mothers' shifts to more, less, and the same level of instruction by comparing correspondence instructions immediately preceding and immediately following children's correspondence errors. We did the same for mothers' sequence instruction following children's sequence errors. In the example above, after each of the child's errors, the mother shifted to more specified instruction and less complex goals. For correspondence instruction, the mother began the task by instructing her child, "Count the dots" (line 1—maternal correspondence scheme: level 0). Following the child's first correspondence error (line 2), she shifted to more specified instruction by providing a specific strategy: "Count the dots in rows" (line 3—maternal correspondence scheme: level 1). Similarly, following the child's second correspondence error (line 8), the mother provided still more specified correspondence instruction: "Now count the dots in the top row" (line 9—maternal correspondence scheme: level 3). The mother provided no sequence instruction until the child made a sequence error:—"five, six, eight" (line 4)—and then asked the child, "What comes after six?" (line 5—maternal sequence scheme: level 1). When the child continued to have difficulty (line 6), the mother gave more specified instruction by providing the next number word: "Seven comes after six" (line 7—maternal sequence scheme: level 5).

Interrater agreement was computed in two steps. First, agreement for children's errors was 84.0%. Then, for those instances in which coders agreed on the existence and type of error, the agreement for the type of shift following the error was 86.8%.

Table 29 contains the mean proportions of maternal shifts following children's correspondence and sequence errors. There were significant effects for the direction of mothers' shift following children's errors (set size 5: following correspondence errors, $F[2,60] = 16.18$, $p < .0001$; following sequence errors, $F[2,42] = 101.53$, $p < .0001$; set size 13: following correspondence errors, $F[2,106] = 48.94$, $p < .0001$; following sequence errors, $F[2,78] = 27.72$, $p < .0001$). Post hoc Duncan's multiple range tests revealed that, following children's errors, mothers tended to shift to more specified instructions. Two additional 2 (age) × 2 (social class) ANOVAs for each set-size condition, one for instruction following children's correspondence errors and one for instruction following children's sequence errors, produced no effects for age or social class.

TABLE 29

MEAN PROPORTIONS OF MOTHER'S SHIFTS IN LEVEL OF INSTRUCTION
FOLLOWING CHILDREN'S ERRORS

| | SHIFT IN MOTHERS' INSTRUCTION | | |
ERROR TYPE	More Specified	No Change	Less Specified
Set 5:			
Correspondence (31)	.67	.28	.05
Sequence (22)	.84	**.11**	**.05**
Set 13:			
Correspondence (54)	.69	.26	.06
Sequence (40)	.61	.31	.08

NOTE.—Proportions do not total 100 because of rounding. Numbers in parentheses represent sample sizes. Adjacent values in boldface type do not differ significantly.

75

Analyses of Children's Adjustments to Maternal Instruction

To examine children's adjustments to their mothers' correspondence and sequence instruction we (*a*) compared children's successful completion of the correspondence and sequence subgoals of the task in their unassisted performances with their success with those subgoals in the interactions and (*b*) analyzed the appropriateness of children's adjustments to maternal number-related directives during the mother-child interactions.

Successful Completion of the Correspondence and Sequence Goals of the Task with and without Maternal Instruction

Table 30 contains the percentage of children who successfully accomplished the correspondence and sequence subgoals of the task in their assisted performances but not in their unassisted performances. Successful accomplishment of the correspondence goals was defined as pointing to each and every dot in the array once and only once (regardless of the correspondence order or whether number words were assigned to dots). A majority of the children in virtually every group who were inaccurate alone did successfully accomplish the subgoals with maternal assistance in both sets. The only exception to this finding is the working-class 2-year-old group for the correspondence subgoals of set 13; however, a substantial proportion (40%) of this group did successfully accomplish this subgoal with maternal assistance. Chi-square analyses revealed no age or social class differ-

TABLE 30

PERCENT DISTRIBUTION OF CHILDREN WHO SUCCESSFULLY ACCOMPLISHED
CORRESPONDENCE OR SEQUENCE GOALS WITH MATERNAL INSTRUCTION BUT NOT ALONE

	SEQUENCE		CORRESPONDENCE	
GROUP	Set 5	Set 13	Set 5	Set 13
Middle class:				
2-year-olds	75	55	73	53
	(15)	(20)	(15)	(19)
4-year-olds	...	75	...	87
	(0)	(8)	(0)	(15)
Working class:				
2-year-olds	64	69	58	40
	(11)	(16)	(12)	(15)
4-year-olds	100	86	...	80
	(4)	(7)	(0)	(15)

NOTE.—Numbers in parentheses indicate total number of children who did not successfully accomplish subgoal without maternal instruction.

ences. (Of the children who did successfully accomplish the subgoals of the task in their unassisted performances, all but one also succeeded with maternal assistance. The one exception was a working-class 2-year-old who successfully accomplished the sequence—but not the correspondence—goals of both sets without assistance but lost interest and quit during the interaction.)

Appropriateness of Children's Adjustments to Maternal Instruction

To examine adjustments in children's goal-directed behaviors in response to maternal instruction, we analyzed children's responses following mothers' correspondence and sequence instruction. Using the coding schemes presented in Tables 22 and 23, children were classified as making appropriate adjustments if more than 50% of their responses to each category of maternal assistance were appropriate. There are two indices of appropriateness: a conservative index containing only adjustments classified as appropriate and a liberal index containing children's partial adjustments as well.

Interrater agreement for coding children's adjustments was computed in two steps. First, agreement for mothers' instructions was 87.4%. Then, for those instances in which coders agreed on the existence and type of maternal instruction, agreement on the type of child adjustment that followed was 93.4%.

The results for adjustments to maternal correspondence instruction are contained in Table 31. For both sets, all groups of children tended to make appropriate adjustments to both general and local correspondence instruction. In contrast, for set 13, few of the 2-year-olds responded appropriately to maternal instruction that focused on using a linear strategy or groups of dots (age differences were significant: strategy conservative index: $\chi^2[1, N = 33] = 9.05, p < .01$; strategy liberal index: $\chi^2[1, N = 34] = 10.81, p < .001$). Appropriately, few mothers of 2-year-olds offered this kind of instruction. There were no other age differences, nor were there any social class differences, in the likelihood of appropriate adjustment.

The results for adjustments to maternal sequence instruction for sets 5 and 13 are contained in Table 32. Regardless of age or social class group, nearly all children tended to respond appropriately to general sequence instruction. For local sequence instruction, few children provided the correct number word (conservative index), although a majority did provide some number word (liberal index). The 4-year-olds were more likely to respond appropriately to general sequence instruction on set 5 than were the 2-year-olds, $\chi^2(1, N = 59) = 6.64, p < .01$. There were no other significant age effects, and there were no social class effects.

TABLE 31

PERCENT DISTRIBUTION OF CHILDREN MAKING APPROPRIATE ADJUSTMENTS TO MATERNAL
CORRESPONDENCE INSTRUCTION—SETS 5 AND 13

| | | TYPE OF INSTRUCTION | | | |
| | | Strategy | | Local | |
GROUP	General	Conservative	Liberal	Conservative	Liberal
Set 5:					
Middle class:					
2-year-olds	94	...	...	67	78
	(16)	...	...	(9)	(9)
4-year-olds	100	...	...	100	100
	(18)	...	...	(1)	(1)
Working class:					
2-year-olds	91	...	...	67	78
	(11)	...	...	(9)	(9)
4-year-olds	94	...	...	83	83
	(17)	...	...	(6)	(6)
Set 13:					
Middle class:					
2-year-olds	100	17	33	55	73
	(13)	(6)	(6)	(11)	(11)
4-year-olds	100	77	93	60	80
	(18)	(13)	(14)	(5)	(5)
Working class:					
2-year-olds	89	0	25	64	91
	(9)	(4)	(4)	(11)	(11)
4-year-olds	93	70	90	90	100
	(15)	(10)	(10)	(10)	(10)

NOTE.—Numbers in parentheses indicate total number of children who received each form of maternal instruction.
Codes for maternal strategy instruction were applied to set 13 only; few mothers used this form of instruction on set 5.

SUMMARY AND DISCUSSION

In this chapter, our concern was to understand the goal structure of a counting activity as it emerged over the course of the interactions of our mother-child pairs. Two complementary sets of analyses were conducted: one of mothers' adjustments in their instruction as a function of children's abilities and task complexity and the other of children's adjustments in their own goal-directed behavior in response to maternal instruction.

In the first set of analyses, three types of maternal instructions were examined, and each produced evidence that mothers did adjust their instruction to children's efforts to accomplish the tasks. (1) Mothers generally recognized the type of difficulty their children were experiencing on the task and responded with instruction tailored to that difficulty: mothers tended to provide correspondence instruction following children's correspondence errors and sequence instruction following children's sequence

TABLE 32

PERCENT DISTRIBUTION OF CHILDREN MAKING APPROPRIATE ADJUSTMENTS TO MATERNAL
SEQUENCE INSTRUCTION—SETS 5 AND 13

	TYPE OF INSTRUCTION					
	Set 5			Set 13		
		Local			Local	
GROUP	General	Conservative	Liberal	General	Conservative	Liberal
Middle class:						
2-year-olds	67	29	71	87	0	71
	(15)	(7)	(7)	(15)	(7)	(7)
4-year-olds	100	...	...	95	33	100
	(17)	(0)	(0)	(20)	(6)	(6)
Working class:						
2-year-olds	73	20	40	82	0	80
	(11)	(5)	(5)	(11)	(5)	(5)
4-year-olds	94	...	...	95	0	100
	(16)	(0)	(0)	(19)	(4)	(4)

NOTE.—Numbers in parentheses indicate total number of children who received each form of maternal instruction.

errors. (2) Following children's errors, mothers shifted to more specified correspondence and sequence instruction. (3) Mothers generally adjusted the overall complexity level of their instruction to children's understanding and the complexity of the task. Mothers of more able children (assessed by their unassisted performance) tended to provide less specified correspondence and sequence instruction than did mothers of less able children. Mothers also tended to provide more specified correspondence and sequence instruction on the larger, more difficult set, except in their introductions to the two sets.

In the second set of analyses, two forms of child adjustments to maternal instruction were examined, and evidence was reported that children generally did adjust their goal-directed activities to their mothers' instruction. (1) The majority of children who had not successfully completed the correspondence and sequence subgoals in their unassisted performances were able to do so with maternal assistance. (2) Children generally made appropriate adjustments to those maternal instructions that focused on task goals, such as requests to count or to count a particular dot.

The findings reviewed indicate that, through their instruction, mothers created contexts in which children were able to utilize their understandings to achieve more complex goals than they could do alone. Two exceptions to this pattern of results highlight the fact that the goal structure of the activity emerges through reciprocal adjustments by mother and child. First, although mothers appropriately provided more specified instruction on the more difficult set-size condition, the specificity of their introductions did not vary across the two sets. Thus, it was through interacting with their children that mothers arrived at an appropriate level of instructional complexity. Second, the only form of maternal instruction to which children did not make appropriate adjustments was instruction in using a linear strategy for set 13: 2-year-olds did not respond appropriately. Correspondingly, relatively few mothers of 2-year-olds provided such instruction. These findings highlight both the regularity with which mothers provided instruction for which children could produce appropriate adjustments and the dependence of children's appropriate adjustments on instruction that meshes with their conceptualizations. Thus, the thrust of our analyses reveals that mothers and children are producing appropriate adjustments to one anothers' adjustments—a phenomenon that leads to an emergent task organization.

The large majority of our analyses produced no social class differences, revealing that all mothers, irrespective of social class, provided appropriate assistance for their children and that all children tended to respond appropriately to maternal instruction. We did, however, find social class differences in mothers' instruction for the correspondence goals of set 13. These findings may provide some support for the large body of research reporting social class differences in maternal teaching styles, indicating that mothers from low social class groups tend to be more directive than their middle-class counterparts are. Alternatively, it may be that both groups of mothers are producing appropriate adjustments to their children's ability to contribute to the correspondence goals on the set 13 task. In support of this alternative, we note that the corespondence goals of set 13 are the most complex aspect of the counting task and that working-class children demonstrated less competence than middle-class children did in their unassisted performances on tasks involving more complex goal structures reported in Chapter III. Though we found no social class differences in children's unassisted performances on the set 13 complex counting task, it is possible that our measure of children's set 13 unassisted correspondence ability failed to capture actual social class differences in children's abilities; if so, mothers in both social class groups were making appropriate adjustments to their children's abilities to contribute to the correspondence goals on set 13.

VII. THE EMERGENT ORGANIZATION OF NUMERICAL ACTIVITIES IN SOCIAL INTERACTIONS: ANALYSES OF A DOUBLE-ARRAY ACTIVITY

In Chapter III, we reported children's unassisted performances on the number reproduction task for two set-size conditions, three and nine elements. Our results indicated that the younger children were less likely than the older children were to reproduce the model set correctly for the small set size, that the middle-class 4-year-olds were more likely to use higher-level reproduction strategies than the middle-class 2-year-olds were, and that the middle-class 4-year-olds were more likely to use higher-level strategies than the working-class 4-year-olds were. These age and social class effects are evidence of differences in children's goals when attempting the number reproduction activity alone: the goals of some children are nonnumerical (level 1), the goals of others are to produce representations of single sets (level 2), and the goals of still others are to reproduce the model set (level 3). The purpose of the present chapter is to understand the way in which the goal structure of the number reproduction activity is adjusted as it emerges in social interactions between children and their mothers.

METHOD

Procedures

Instructions to mothers.—Mothers were given a board containing pictures of either three or nine Cookie Monsters (the model set) and a cup and were told:

I would like you and your child to sit on the floor with a board like this. Over to the side, there will be another board with several pennies on it [the available set]. The object of the game is for your child to put in the cup the same number of pennies as there are Cookie Monsters on the board. You can do it however you like, but your child has to get up and go over to the pennies with the cup—you cannot move them all closer to the Cookie Monster board. Once your child has done this, empty the cup and repeat the game—this time using the other Cookie Monster board. Please remember to empty the pennies from the cup before you start the second board. Remember, some children need more help than others, but what we are interested in is the sort of help and guidance you provide so that your child might learn something about numbers in playing the game.

We situated the child facing the mother, and we placed the pile of pennies about 4 feet to the rear of the child (see Fig. 2).

Coding

The schemes for coding were based on a detailed task analysis. The complete coding schemes are available from the first author.

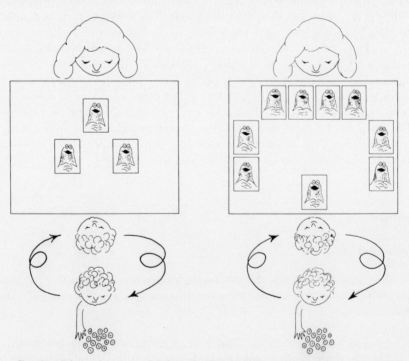

Fig. 2.—Schematic portrayals of set size 3 (left) and set size 9 (right) number reproduction activities.

Task analysis.—The superordinate goal of the task is to retrieve the same number of pennies as Cookie Monsters. The organization of a prototypical task solution contains three task phases during which the superordinate goal is accomplished.

1. *Model-set phase.*—In order to achieve the superordinate goal of the task, an individual must first achieve an accurate numerical representation of the model set. One means of achieving this goal is to count the model set, and, in order to achieve an accurate count, further subgoals must be identified and accomplished (e.g., to assign one and only one number word from the conventional sequence to each Cookie Monster).

2. *Available-set phase.*—To produce a numerical copy of the model set, an individual must accomplish a sequence of subgoals in the available-set phase similar to those already accomplished in the model-set phase. For instance, the individual must count a set of pennies to the same number achieved in counting the model set. To accomplish this subgoal, the individual must, again, assign number words in one-to-one correspondence to the targeted objects, this time stopping when the value of the enumeration is equivalent to the number of Cookie Monsters.

3. *Check phase.*—The individual may choose to check his or her numerical reproduction for accuracy. To accomplish such a check, an individual would generate another set of subgoals. For instance, one approach would be to establish a one-to-one correspondence between the pennies in the cup and the Cookie Monsters in the model set. Another approach would entail a count of the pennies and a count of the Cookie Monsters.

Organization of coding schemes.—The task phases were identified by the following criteria. The model-set phase contained the dyad's accomplishment of a numerical representation of the model set (e.g., counting the Cookie Monsters) as well as utterances assisting the transition to the available set (e.g., the mother saying, "Go get the same number of pennies"). The available-set phase contained activity involving the available set (the pennies). The check phase contained activities that followed the available-set phase and that were organized to determine whether the task had been accomplished (e.g., one-to-one correspondences and recounting pennies).

These phases constituted different contexts for mothers' instruction and for children's adaptations to their mothers' instruction. As will be outlined in subsequent sections, we constructed separate coding schemes for mothers' instruction and children's adaptations within the model-set and the available-set phases, and we used these schemes to produce our primary results. We produced a more global analysis of dyads' organizations of check phases. (This phase was not required in our instructions to mothers, and, therefore, variations in its organization were more difficult to interpret.)

1. *Model-set phase codes.*—Model-set phase codes consisted of three types: children's accuracy, dyads' success in accomplishing the numerical represen-

tation of the model set, and mothers' instruction that served to structure and restructure the goals of the task.

a) Children's accuracy (counts and judgments).—A count was defined as a sequence of one or more numbers beginning with "one" with or without accompanying gestures and with or without maternal instruction. A judgment was defined as a statement of the numerosity of the set without any immediately preceding count (e.g., child simply looks at set 3 board and says, "Three"). Each attempted count or judgment of the model was coded for its accuracy (correct/incorrect).

b) Dyads' success in the model-set phase.—The success of each dyad's activity (as distinct from the individual child's activity) was coded to distinguish two different emergent contexts of mothers' instruction: (1) successful, indicating that a correct count or judgment of the entire model set was achieved during the model-set phase (whether or not incorrect counts or judgments preceded it), and (2) unsuccessful, indicating that a correct count or judgment of the model set was not achieved.

c) Maternal instruction.—Maternal instruction during the model-set phase was coded with two schemes, one for task simplifications and one for specificity of instruction.

Task simplification was coded if a mother transformed the goal structure of the task into a nonnumerical structure (e.g., a mother might request, "Go get a penny for this Cookie Monster," or, "Go get some pennies"). A simplification was coded for its first point of occurrence in the interaction: mother's introduction to the task, during the model-set phase, the available-set phase, the check phase, or any other subsequent interaction.[7]

Specificity of instruction was coded with a scheme consisting of an ordered set of 11 levels, in which lowest-numbered levels indicate formulation of the double-array (superordinate) goal (e.g., "Okay, what we're going to do is get pennies for these Cookie Monsters, the same number of pennies as there are Cookie Monsters on this board"), intermediate levels reflect single-array subgoals (e.g., "How many Cookie Monsters are there here?"), and highest-numbered levels reflect progressively more specified subgoal instruction in counting (e.g., "Start with one: one, two . . ."). Table 33 contains a description of these levels.[8] On the basis of this scheme, we constructed seven

---

[7] In addition to check phases, there were occasional repetitions of the task (i.e., the same set) initiated by mother or child. These were unusual: only three dyads in set 3 and nine dyads in set 9 repeated.

[8] Maternal instruction was coded for the presence of each level of instruction it contained. Thus, e.g., "Count these" is level 5, while "Count these so you'll know how many Cookie Monsters there are" is both level 5 and level 4. A given maternal level could be coded only once for each child count or judgment (or for any model-set phase without any count or judgment). A model-set phase could, however, contain more than one count or judgment, and the constraint on coding the same level more than once did not apply across counts and/or judgments.

TABLE 33

A HIERARCHICAL ORDERING OF MATERNAL INSTRUCTIONS FOR THE MODEL-SET PHASE
OF THE NUMBER REPRODUCTION TASK

Maternal Instruction Level	Example
Instructions pertaining to the goal structure of the entire task:	
1. Mother provides the superordinate goal of the entire task	"Get just the same number of pennies as Cookie Monsters."
2. Mother provides the superordinate goal of the entire task after a representation of the model set has been accomplished	"Get just the same number of pennies as Cookie Monsters."
Instructions linking a representation of the model set with a production of a copy:	
3. Mother instructs the child to retrieve a specified number (three or nine) from the available set	"Go get nine pennies for the Cookie Monsters."
Instructions to produce a representation of the model set:	
4. Mother instructs child to produce a representation of the model set without specifying how to do so ...	"How many Cookie Monsters are there?"
5. Mother instructs child to produce a representation of the model set and specifies a procedure whereby this can be accomplished	"Count the Cookie Monsters."
6–10. Mother provides increasing instruction on some aspect of the child's counting activity with each successive level	Mother counts as child points to each Cookie Monster.
Instruction providing a representation of the model set:	
11. Mother provides a cardinal representation of the model set for the child	"There are three Cookie Monsters."

measures to analyze the emergent goal structure of model-set phase activity.

Four measures provided indices of the specificity of the mother's instruction in the model-set phase. (1) Median level of instruction is the median of all maternal instruction codes assigned to a given model-set phase. It is the most general measure of maternal instruction in that it was based on all maternal instruction codes assigned to each model-set phase. Thus, if a mother instructed at level 4 for one count, levels 5 and 8 for a second count, and levels 6 and 9 for a third count and ended the model-set phase with levels 3 and 2, the measure would be the median levels of 2, 3, 4, 5, 6, 8, and

9, which is level 5. (2) Most specified instruction is the level of instruction for each model-set phase that was assigned the highest-numbered subgoal. In the example above, the measure is level 9. (3) Mothers' explanation of the superordinate goal was determined by the presence of instruction at levels 1 or 2, the superordinate goal level. This measure indicated mothers' concern to explain to their children the goal of the task. In the example above, the mother is coded for explanation of the superordinate (level 2). (4) Mothers' last instruction in the model-set phase provided a measure of the specificity with which mothers assisted children's transition to the available-set phase: we coded whether mothers specified the number of pennies to retrieve (e.g., "Now get three pennies") or not.

We used three measures to reveal regularities in the way the goal structure of the activity shifted over the course of the model-set phase interactions. We expected that, when children were doing well, their mothers would relinquish responsibility for constructing the subgoals of the task to them and, thus, instruct with less specificity and that, when children were having difficulties, mothers would structure subgoals with greater degrees of specificity. Therefore, we analyzed the relation of maternal instruction before and after children's correct counts (or judgments) and before and after children's incorrect counts (or judgments). Shifts to more specified instruction, shifts to less specified instruction, and no change in level of instruction were examined for correct versus incorrect counts in each set size.

2. *Available-set phase codes.*—For the available-set phase interactions, we developed coding schemes for children's counts, dyads' success, and maternal instruction that were similar to those for the model-set phase interactions. We coded existence and accuracy of children's counts and dyads' success with the same schemes used in the model-set phase. Specificity of maternal instruction in the available-set phase was coded with an ordered scheme parallel to that for maternal instruction in the model-set phase, and two measures were derived as indices of the specificity of the task organization: median level of instruction and most specified instruction.

3. *Check phase codes.*—Check phase codes were based on our analyses of developmental shifts in children's goals and means (see Table 8). Thus, level 3 check phases were those in which a single-array activity was related to the double-array goal. For instance, the child might count or produce a number judgment of the pennies or Cookie Monsters, and then the mother and child might discuss the numerical relation between the set of pennies and the set of Cookie Monsters or establish a one-to-one correspondence between the pennies and the Cookie Monsters. Level 2 check phases were those in which the dyads constructed single-array goals but in which the double-array goal was not explicit: either pennies were placed in one-to-one correspondence with no accompanying verbalization indicating the relevance of the corre-

spondence to numerical reproduction, or the pennies were recounted with no verbalization or activity indicating the relevance of that count to the double-array reproduction goal. There were no check phases that contained only level 1 activities. However, some dyads did not organize a check phase, so *no check phase* was coded if the child returned with pennies, and there was no further task-relevant comment or task activity for that set size by the mother or the child.

Intercoder agreements.—One of us coded 100% of the videotapes, and a second rater independently coded a random sample of 20% of the videotapes equally distributed across age and social class groups. Several procedures were used for the determination of intercoder agreements.

Specificity of mothers' instruction (e.g., median level or most specified maternal instruction) was examined only for successful model-set phases, and, therefore, as the condition for the applicability of the specificity measure, calculation of rater agreement necessarily excluded data from any subject for whom the raters had not first agreed on dyad's success. Therefore, we calculated agreements in two steps: first, the percent agreement on the applicability of a given measure (whether the dyad was successful) and, second, the Pearson correlation coefficient of the measures derived from each rater's raw codings. Similarly, measures of mother's shifts in model-set phase instruction after correct versus incorrect counts/judgments were computed for each count/judgment, and, again, computation of agreement necessarily excluded subjects for whom the coders had not agreed on the applicability of the measure (i.e., presence of correct count or judgment or presence of an incorrect count or judgment). Again, calculation of agreements was conducted in two steps: first, the percent agreement on the applicability of a given measure (e.g., whether the child counted correctly) and, second, the percent agreement on each coder's measure of mother's shift in specificity of instruction (e.g., shift up, shift down, or no change). Agreements for all other measures were computed as percent agreements.

Agreements are contained in Table 34. Agreements for our measures ranged from moderate to high (note that all correlations are greater than 0.90 and that 13 of 26 agreements were above 90%).

Index of Children's Unassisted Performance

As a measure of children's spontaneous goals in the reproduction activity, we constructed a composite index on the basis of children's performances in both set 3 and set 9 of the unassisted version of the reproduction task (see Chap. III). The index consisted of a four-point ordinal scale reflecting progressively greater ability to structure reproduction goals for the activity and to accomplish the goals successfully: (1) children did not succeed on either set and used no visible counting activity when attempting

TABLE 34

RELIABILITIES FOR MEASURES USED IN ANALYSES OF DYADS' PERFORMANCES IN
ASSISTED REPRODUCTION TASKS

| | PERCENT AGREEMENT | | PEARSON CORRELATIONS | |
MEASURE	Set 3	Set 9	Set 3	Set 9
Model-set phase:				
Dyads' success	.94	.94	...	...
Median level of instruction	...	...	.98	.94
Most specified instruction	...	...	.99	.95
Mothers' explanation of superordinate	1.00	.94	...	...
Mothers' last instruction	.94	.89	...	...
Mothers' shifts in instruction:				
Correct:				
Applicability	1.00	.94	...	...
Shift:				
Up	1.00	.92	...	...
Down	.81	.85	...	...
None	.81	.92	...	...
Incorrect:				
Applicability	.83	.94	...	...
Shift:				
Up	.67	.75	...	...
Down	1.00	.63	...	...
None	.67	.75	...	...
Available-set phase:				
Dyads' success	.72	.89	...	...
Median level of instruction	...	...	.91	1.00
Most specified instruction	...	...	.95	1.00
Check phase:				
Type...	.94	.89	...	...
Other:				
Simplifications	.89	.94	...	...
Recycles	.94	.89	...	...

set 9; (2) children succeeded on set 3, but on set 9 they did not succeed and used no visible counting activity; (3) children succeeded on set 3, but on set 9 they did not succeed, although they used some counting on one or both sets; (4) children succeeded on both set 3 and set 9, using either a trial-and-error or a systematic counting strategy for set 9.

This measure of children's unassisted performance correlated with age for both social class groups (middle class, $r = .66$, $p < .001$; working class, $r = .46$, $p < .01$). The measure correlated with social class only for the 4-year-olds ($r = .31$, $p < .05$; middle-class 4-year-olds had higher scores than did working-class 4-year-olds). This association between children's unassisted performance and social class would make interpretation of any significant associations between measures of maternal instruction and social class problematic, in that associations between maternal instruction and social class could arise from one of two sources: social class differences in the way mothers organize the reproduction activity or maternal adjustments of the task organization to social class differences in their children's abilities. In order to examine the relation between maternal instruction and social class, it was, therefore, necessary to control for social class differences in children's ability. To accomplish this, we computed second-order partial correlations between measures of maternal instruction and social class with both measures of children's ability (age and unassisted performance) partialed out.

RESULTS

Our analysis of the organization of the number reproduction activity over the course of dyadic interactions consists of four components: (1) analyses of dyads' emergent success in the model-set and available-set phases, (2) analyses of mothers' adjustments to their children's abilities in the model-set and available-set phases, (3) analyses of children's adjustments to their mothers' instruction in the model-set and available-set phases, and (4) an additional, less detailed analysis of dyads' organizations of check phases.

Dyads' Emergent Success in the Model-Set and Available-Set Phases

Not all dyads succeeded in accomplishing an accurate representation of the model set in the model-set phase or a reproduction of the model set in the available-set phase. Table 35 contains the correlations, for sets 3 and 9, of dyads' success in each phase with children's unassisted performance, children's age, and social class. In the model-set phases of both sets, children's ability as indexed by age was related to dyads' success. When children were assisted by their mothers, older children were more likely to achieve an accurate numerical representation than were younger children. In the available-set phases of both sets, both indices of children's ability were related to dyads' success. When assisted by their mothers, older and/or more able children were more likely to reproduce the model set in the available-set phase. Task difficulty (set size) was also related to dyads' success in the available-set phase. About one-third of the dyads differed in success across sets (23 of 67 dyads); of these, more succeeded only on set 3 than only on set 9 ($N = 23$, $p = .0347$, binomial test). Social class was not related to dyads' success in either task phase of either set.

Not all dyads were able to complete this double-array activity together, especially in set 9. It appears that a child needed some minimal level of ability for he or she and the mother to adjust to one another's contributions to the double-array task. Because our goal was to examine the emergent goal structure of the double-array activity, in many of our analyses we included only successful dyads in which both mother and child were truly contribut-

TABLE 35

PEARSON CORRELATION COEFFICIENTS OF DYADS' SUCCESS IN MODEL-SET AND
AVAILABLE-SET PHASES WITH CHILDREN'S UNASSISTED PERFORMANCE,
AGE, AND SOCIAL CLASS

Phase	Unassisted Performance	Age	SES[a]	SES. Unassisted Performance, Age[b]
Set 3:				
Model set (70)	.14	.30**	.16	.18
Available set (70)	.49***	.51***	.07	.03
Set 9:				
Model set (73)	.19	.44***	.01	.03
Available set (72)	.27*	.32**	.02	.00

NOTE.—Numbers in parentheses represent sample sizes.

[a] Working class = 1; middle class = 2.

[b] The correlation between dyads' success and social class, controlling for unassisted performance and age group.

* $p < .05$.

** $p < .01$.

*** $p < .001$.

ing to the double-array goal. We excluded dyads if children were never successful or if mothers had simplified the activity to a level 1 (nonnumerical) activity. We recognize that many analyses are, therefore, limited to more able subjects. Appendix C contains parallel analyses of excluded subjects.

Mothers' Adjustments to Children's Performance

Simplifications

Table 36 contains correlations of mothers' use of simplifications with children's unassisted performance, age, and social class for each set size. Correlations were produced for simplifications coded at four different points in the interactions: (1) initially; (2) any time up through the model-set phase, including 1; (3) any time up through the available-set phase, including 1 and 2; and (4) any time during the entire task, including 1, 2, and 3. If the correlations between either of our ability indices and maternal simplifications were larger at later points in the interactions than at earlier points, such a pattern would indicate that mothers' use of simplification as an adjustment to children's abilities tended to emerge during the interaction, after mothers observed their children's difficulties. In both sets, mothers' use of simplifications was increasingly related to children's ability (as indexed by both unassisted performance and age). Mothers of less able and younger children were more likely to simplify at any time during the task than mothers of more able and older children were, and mothers' use of

TABLE 36

<small>PEARSON CORRELATION COEFFICIENTS OF MATERNAL SIMPLIFICATIONS UP THROUGH 4
POINTS IN THE INTERACTIONS WITH CHILDREN'S UNASSISTED PERFORMANCE,
AGE, AND SOCIAL CLASS</small>

Points of Simplification	Unassisted Performance	Age	SES[a]	SES. Unassisted Performance, Age[b]
Set 3:				
Initial (3, 72)	−.09	−.08	−.22*	−.22*
Through model set (6, 72)	−.10	−.18	−.18	−.20‡
Through available set (9, 72) ...	−.14	−.29**	−.11	−.14
Entire task (11, 72)	−.19†	−.35**	−.11	−.13
Set 9:				
Initial (6, 74)	−.07	−.21*	−.02	−.04
Through model set (14, 74)	−.21*	−.40***	−.07	−.10
Through available set (18, 74) ..	−.23*	−.38***	−.07	−.08
Entire task (25, 74)	−.24*	−.38***	−.11	−.12

NOTE.—Numbers in parentheses indicate number of mothers who simplified and number of dyads that attempted the number reproduction activity.

[a] Working class = 1; middle class = 2.

[b] The correlation between maternal simplification and social class, controlling for unassisted performance and age group.

* $p < .05$.
** $p < .01$.
*** $p < .001$.
† $p = .056$.
‡ $p = .051$.

simplification (as an adjustment to children's abilities) tended to emerge during the interactions. Social class was related to mothers' use of simplification only for initial use in set 3 and remained so when age and unassisted performance were partialed out. In set 3, working-class mothers were more likely to simplify the task immediately than were middle-class mothers. However, there were no social class differences in the overall use of simplification across all phases of the interactions.

Model-Set Phase

Specificity of mothers' instruction during successful model-set phases.—Table 37 contains the correlations of mothers' specificity in successful model-set phases with children's unassisted performance, age, and social class for each set size. Unassisted performance was related to each of the four measures of maternal specificity in both sets. Child's age was related to each of the measures in both sets, with the exception of mothers' formulation of the superordinate in set 9. Each of the significant correlations indicates that, in successful model-set phases, mothers used more specified instruction for less able or younger children. Social class was related to two measures of

TABLE 37

Maternal Instruction	Unassisted Performance	Age	SES[a]	SES. Unassisted Performance, Age[b]
Set 3:				
Median level (56)	−.28*	−.52***	−.26*	−.32**
Most specified (59)	−.39**	−.61***	−.22*	−.27*
Superordinate (58)	.30*	.45***	−.04	.01
Last instruction (58)	−.29*	−.49***	−.06	−.05
Set 9:				
Median level (52)	−.43**	−.30*	−.06	.05
Most specified (55)	−.56***	−.57***	−.11	.01
Superordinate (56)	.23*	.07	−.02	−.01
Last instruction (55)	−.32**	−.32**	.00	−.07

NOTE.—Numbers in parentheses represent sample sizes.

[a] Working class = 1; middle class = 2.

[b] The correlation between maternal instruction and social class, controlling for unassisted performance and age group.

* $p < .05$.

** $p < .01$.

*** $p < .001$.

maternal instruction—median level and most specified instruction—in set 3 only, and it remained so when both indices of ability were partialed out. In set 3, working-class mothers used more specified instruction in successful model-set phases than did middle-class mothers.[9]

Shifts in instruction after correct versus incorrect counts or judgments in the model-set phase.—To analyze shifts in the specificity of mothers' instruction, we computed the mean proportion of shifts to more, less, and the same level of instruction following both correct and incorrect counts or judgments. Included as subjects for each ANOVA were, for each set size, either those subjects who had ever attempted a count that resulted in an incorrect solution (incorrect) or those subjects who had achieved a successful count (correct). In order to determine whether there were age and social class differences in the probability of predicted shifts in each set (shifts to less specificity after correct counts and shifts to greater specificity after incorrect counts), we performed a set of four 2 (age) × 2 (social class) ANOVAs (shifts following set 3 correct counts, set 3 incorrect counts, set 9 correct counts, and set 9 incorrect counts). The ANOVAs produced no main effects or interactions. The means can be found in Table 38. All mothers, regardless of child's age

[9] The partial correlations for social class and maternal instruction are slightly greater than our zero-order correlations since age, in that it is uncorrelated with social class and correlated with maternal instruction, acts as a suppressor variable (Pedhazur, 1982).

TABLE 38

MEAN PROPORTION OF PREDICTED SHIFTS IN MATERNAL INSTRUCTION FOLLOWING BOTH
CORRECT AND INCORRECT COUNTS OR JUDGMENTS IN SETS 3 AND 9

| | SET 3 | | | | SET 9 | | | |
| | Middle Class | | Working Class | | Middle Class | | Working Class | |
AGE GROUP AND ACCURACY	N	M	N	M	N	M	N	M
2-year-olds:								
Incorrect	6	.83	7	.72	9	.73	8	.49
Correct	15	.87	12	.82	11	.86	10	1.00
4-year-olds:								
Incorrect	2	.50	4	1.00	7	.63	10	.80
Correct	18	.83	15	.81	19	.89	15	.77

or dyad's social class, were equally likely to make the predicted shift in instructional specificity after both correct and incorrect counts.

Because there were no age or social class differences in the probability of predicted shift, we collapsed age and social class classifications in order to examine whether the predicted shift was indeed the most likely shift (using one-way, repeated-measures ANOVAs). Table 39 contains the means and results from these analyses. An effect of shift type was obtained for each analysis. Post hoc Scheffé comparisons between pairs of shift types indicated that, as expected, mothers tended to shift to less specified instruction following a correct count and that mothers tended to shift to more specified instruction following an incorrect count ($p < .05$).

TABLE 39

F AND p VALUES AND MEANS FOR TYPE OF MATERNAL SHIFT FOR CORRECT AND
INCORRECT COUNTS OR JUDGMENTS IN SETS 3 AND 9

| | | | SHIFT TYPE | | |
SET: CORRECT	F	N	Increase	Same	Decrease
Set 3:					
Incorrect	39.38* (3,15)	19	.79	**.17**	**.06**
Correct	133.03* (3,56)	60	**.07**	**.09**	.83
Set 9:					
Incorrect	23.87* (3,30)	34	.68	**.19**	**.13**
Correct	181.61* (3,51)	55	**.07**	**.06**	.87

NOTE.—Numbers in parentheses represent degrees of freedom. Adjacent means in boldface type do not differ significantly.
* $p < .0001$.

TABLE 40

PEARSON CORRELATION COEFFICIENTS OF MATERNAL INSTRUCTION IN SUCCESSFUL
AVAILABLE-SET PHASES WITH CHILDREN'S UNASSISTED PERFORMANCE,
AGE, AND SOCIAL CLASS

Maternal Instruction	Unassisted Performance	Age	SES[a]	SES. Unassisted Performance, Age[b]
Set 3:				
Median level (42)	−.40**	−.65***	−.09	.02
Most specified (42)	−.37**	−.73***	−.07	.04
Set 9:				
Median level (29)	−.72***	−.56**	−.32*	−.21
Most specified (29)	−.57**	−.45**	−.36*	−.27

NOTE.—Numbers in parentheses represent sample sizes.
[a] Working class = 1; middle class = 2.
[b] The correlation between maternal instruction and social class, controlling for unassisted performance and age group.
* $p < .05$.
** $p < .01$.
*** $p < .001$.

Available-Set Phase

Specificity of maternal instruction in successful available-set phases.—Table 40 contains Pearson correlations, for sets 3 and 9, of maternal specificity in successful available-set phases with children's unassisted performance, age, and social class. In both sets, both indices of children's ability were related to both measures of maternal instruction. In successful available-set phases, mothers used more specified instruction for less able and younger children. Social class was related to maternal instruction only in set 9, but it did not remain related when variance due to age and unassisted performance was partialed out.

Effects of Set Size (Task Complexity) on the Specificity of Maternal Instruction in the Model-Set and Available-Set Phases

Differences in the specificity of maternal instruction as a function of set size were examined using sign tests. These findings indicate that mothers were making instructional adjustments to the difficulty of the task for their children. Some mothers simplified only in the larger set size: of the 14 mothers who completed both sets and simplified in only one set, 12 did so only in set 9 ($p = .019$, binomial test). For the dyads who were successful in both sets, most of these mothers instructed with greater specificity in set 9 than in set 3: 29 of 39 mothers had greater median levels of specificity for set 9 ($z = 3.08, p < .005$); 38 of 45 mothers had greater most specified levels for set 9 ($z = 4.47$, $p < .0001$); and 12 of 16 mothers had more specified last instructions for set 9 ($p = .038$, binomial). Mothers were not more likely to explain the task goal in the model-set phase as a function of set size; nor were they more likely to use more specified instruction in the available-set phase as a function of set size.

Children's Adjustments to Their Mothers' Instruction

To examine children's adjustments to their mothers' instruction during the reproduction task, we compared both children's use of counting and task success in their unassisted and assisted performances. The results of these analyses are contained in Table 41. Subjects represented in the table are those who completed both the unassisted and the assisted tasks for a given set size and who were unsuccessful on the unassisted task. An additional criterion for inclusion in the counting analysis was absence of immediate maternal simplifications in the assisted model-set phase (if mother simplifies, she never requests a count). An additional criterion for inclusion in the success analysis was absence of any maternal simplifications in the

TABLE 41

PERCENT OF CHILDREN WHO COUNTED AND SUCCEEDED IN THE NUMBER REPRODUCTION TASKS WITH MATERNAL INSTRUCTION BUT NOT WITHOUT

| | | SUCCEEDED[b] | |
GROUP	COUNTED: SET 9[a]	Set 3	Set 9
Middle class:			
2-year-olds	72	42	40
	(18)	(12)	(10)
4-year-olds	100	80	67
	(9)	(5)	(15)
Working class:			
2-year-olds	64	33	57
	(18)	(9)	(7)
4-year-olds	92	43	69
	(13)	(7)	(13)

[a] Numbers in parentheses indicate the total number of children who did not count in their unassisted performance. There were children excluded from this analysis either because they counted when unassisted (10 middle-class and four working-class 4-year-olds) or because their mothers simplified the task immediately so that counting was never requested (two middle-class 2-year-olds and one working-class 4-year-old). All the 4-year-olds who counted without maternal instruction in their unassisted performances also counted with maternal instruction.

[b] Numbers in parentheses indicate number of children who did not successfully accomplish the reproduction task in their unassisted performance. There were subjects excluded from this analysis if (1) they were successful without maternal instruction and unsuccessful with maternal instruction (set 3: two middle-class 2-year-olds and one working-class 4-year-old; set 9: one middle-class 2-year-old), (2) they were successful both without and with maternal instruction (set 3: 15 middle-class 4-year-olds, one working-class 2-year-old, and eight working-class 4-year-olds; set 9: two middle-class 4-year-olds and one working-class 4-year-old), or (3) their mothers simplified the task at some point so that success was no longer requested (set 3: three middle-class 2-year-olds and five middle-class 4-year-olds; set 9: eight middle-class 2-year-olds, two middle-class 4-year-olds, eight working-class 2-year-olds, and four working-class 4-year-olds).

model-set and available-set phases (if mother eventually simplifies, she no longer requests success).

We compared children's unassisted and assisted uses of counting only on set 9 since set 3 can be accomplished successfully without overt counting. Across groups, 61%–100% of those children who did not count when unassisted did at least some counting (either of the model set or of both model and available sets) when assisted by the mother. The 4-year-olds in this analysis were more likely to shift to counting with their mothers than were the 2-year-olds ($p = .026$, Fisher exact test). (All subjects who counted in their unassisted performances also counted with their mothers; see table 41, n. a.)

We compared children's unassisted and assisted task success on both set sizes. For this analysis, success was defined as an accurate reproduction of the model set. The proportion of children in each population group who were not successful without assistance and who were successful with assistance ranged from 33% to 80% on set 3 and from 40% to 69% on set 9. Fisher exact tests revealed no age or social class differences. (Of those children who were successful when unassisted, 24 of 27 in set 3 and three of four in set 9 were also successful when assisted by their mothers; see table 41, n. b.)

Results from the analyses of both shifts in counting and shifts in success indicate that many children were adjusting their activity to their mothers' instruction and were functioning at a higher level with instruction than they were without instruction.

Additional Analysis: Check Phases

Most dyads organized a check phase in each set (in set 3, 66 of 71 dyads; and in set 9, 68 of 69 dyads). Of those that did, between 75% and 85% of the dyads in each age and social class group organized a level 3 check phase in which an effort was made to relate a single-array subgoal (a count or a judgment of one or both sets) to the double-array, superordinate task goal (a discussion of equivalence and/or establishment of one-to-one correspondence).

Level 3 check phases emerged even when mothers had simplified the task earlier in the interaction. (In set 3, of the nine dyads whose mothers simplified, seven then organized a level 3 check phase; in set 9, of the 22 dyads whose mothers simplified, 16 organized a level 3 check phase.) Thus, most mothers' use of simplification as an instructional strategy in the model-set and available-set phases preceded later efforts to assist their children to recognize the reproduction goal. Such check phase instruction can be interpreted as another kind of simplification: because mother and child had the pennies at the board (obviating the need for separate model-set and available-set phases), it was far easier to help the child begin to recognize the goal of the task by helping him or her count and place the pennies in one-to-one correspondence simultaneously.

SUMMARY AND DISCUSSION

Our concern in this chapter was to understand the goal structure of a numerical reproduction activity as it emerged in the course of the dyadic interactions of our mother-child pairs. We expected to find that mothers would adjust their instructions downward to their children's ability to generate and accomplish the goals of the reproduction activity and that children would adjust their participation upward to their mothers' instruction, results similar to those obtained in Chapter VI.

Findings were consistent with our expectations. Mothers made adjustments to their children's abilities in both set sizes. Mothers of less able children were more likely to simplify the task, more likely to provide instruction at lower levels of goal complexity, and less likely to formulate the superordinate goal than were mothers of more able children. The relation between children's ability and mothers' simplifications in the number reproduction task tended to emerge over the course of the interactions, indicating that, through interacting with their children, mothers arrived at an appropriate level of instruction. This result is analogous to findings reported in Chapter VI regarding the lack of child ability–related differences in mothers' introductions and the later appearance of child ability–related differences in maternal instruction during the activity.

Mothers also adjusted their instruction depending on the abilities of their children to attempt the task at different levels of complexity. Mothers were more likely to provide instruction of greater specificity in the model-set phase of the more difficult task (set 9 vs. set 3) and to simplify the more difficult task.

Just as mothers adjusted to their children's abilities, children adjusted their task participation to their mothers' instruction. Many children who were not successful in reproducing one or both set-size conditions alone did so with their mothers' instruction. Many children who did not count spontaneously when attempting to reproduce the larger set alone did so with their mothers. This change in performance was far more common for the 4-year-olds, a change that reflects both the differences in mothers' instructions for the two age groups and the differences in the capacities of the two groups to comply with those instructions. As we found in Chapter VI, the results in this chapter indicate that mothers' instruction created contexts in which children could utilize their understandings to achieve, with assistance, more complex goals.

There was some evidence that mothers' adjustments differed as a function of their social class. In set 3, working-class mothers were more likely than middle-class mothers were to simplify at the beginning of the task and to use more specified instruction in the model-set phase, even when children's abilities were statistically controlled. As noted in Chapter VI, either these results may be analogous to findings reported from previous research that working-class and lower-class mothers are more directive than middle-class mothers when teaching their children, or they may be indicative of some degree of insensitivity in our measure of children's unassisted performance on the set 3 reproduction task: if the measure failed to detect existing social class differences in children's abilities for set 3, then it may be that all mothers were, indeed, making appropriate adjustments to their children's abilities. It is important to note that these relations between socioeconomic status and specificity of instruction were not found for most of our measures. We did not find the same relations in set 9; nor did we find, at either set size, social class relations with other measures of mothers' instruction—explanations of the task goal, specificity of last instruction, or specificity of instruction in the available-set phase.

Several analyses produced no significant relations between social class, age, and unassisted performances and any of our major variables of study. We interpret the pattern of nonsignificant findings as evidence of the stable characteristics of mother-child teaching-learning interactions in the number reproduction task: mothers generally offered instruction at more specified subgoal levels to children of lower levels of competence, mothers generally shifted to less specified instruction after their children succeeded on a count or judgment of an array and to more specified instruction when their children did not succeed, and children usually adjusted to their mothers' instruction by counting when they had not done so alone.

Across Chapters VI and VII, there were correspondences in the results for the complex counting and number reproduction tasks. The organizations of the environments that emerged in the interactions were negotiated ones, ones in which mothers adjusted the task organization in accord with their children's efforts to achieve task goals and ones in which children adjusted their goal-directed behavior to their mothers' instruction.

INTRODUCTION TO PART 5

The final two chapters of this *Monograph* provide an integration of the three components in our treatment of social and developmental processes in children's understandings. In Chapter III, focusing on the developmental component, we were concerned with developmental shifts in children's numerical understandings and produced evidence of the shifting relations between children's generation of numerical forms and numerical functions. In Chapter V, addressing the sociocultural component, we focused on dyads' involvement with everyday number activities and reported their considerable interest and involvement with such activities as well as a correspondence between children's numerical understandings and the goal structure of the activities with which they are engaged. Finally, in Chapters VI and VII, focusing on the social interactional component, we studied mother-child interactions during number activities and demonstrated the negotiated character of children's numerical goals as these emerge in such social interactions. Still missing in our results is an integrative, longitudinal analysis of how shifts over time in the emergent organization of sociocultural activities are related to form-function shifts in children's early number development. This analysis is presented in Chapter VIII. In Chapter IX, we present our conclusions. We set our treatment of social and developmental processes in children's numerical understandings in the context of other treatments, focusing our discussion of the role of socially organized experience in models of cognitive development.

VIII. CONTINUITIES AND DISCONTINUITIES IN SOCIALLY ORGANIZED NUMBER ACTIVITIES DURING EARLY DEVELOPMENT

In this chapter, we focus on two aspects of activity organization related to form-function shifts—continuities and discontinuities in the goal structure of children's socially organized numerical activities.

Continuities in organization include use of the same activity over time, the maintenance of the same teaching goals, and quantitative increases or decreases in dimensions of play such as shifts in the set size or the amount of assistance for the same teaching goals. Such continuities provide children with occasions to specialize developing forms to serve already acquired functions. For instance, the occasional repetition over a several month period of counting stairs is a context for a child to elaborate more adequate means to achieve number word sequence (level 1) and single-array representation (level 2) goals. Increases in the number of stairs counted and/or decreases in maternal guidance would enable the child to specialize knowledge of the number word sequence further and to work toward independence in deploying the emerging numerical forms.

Discontinuities in the organization of play include shifts in the goal structure of an activity over time and the emergence of new teaching goals for an activity. Such discontinuities provide children with the opportunity to use previously acquired forms to accomplish newly emerging functions. For instance, the introduction of an arithmetic goal in climbing stairs, in which the child counts three steps and then must add an additional two, constitutes a discontinuity in the goal structure of the stair-counting activity.

The interplay between continuities and discontinuities over time in the social organization of play is, thus, the social complement of form-function shifts in children's early number development. The question we pursue here is the extent to which such continuities and discontinuities are apparent over the course of early number development.

To gather longitudinal information on the shifting organization of children's numerical activities during early development, we asked mothers to trace the character of play with two of their everyday number activities— one that they considered "easy" for their children and one that they considered "difficult." In the interview, mothers answered questions concerned with the current, past, and projected organization of each activity.

There are problems with the longitudinal self-report method used that we have made efforts to address. While mothers' reports about the character of current and past play are subject to minimal bias since they are grounded in actual experiences with their children, their reports about projected play are less reliable. Mothers undoubtedly differ not only in their ability to anticipate what kinds of play they will be engaged in with their children several months in the future but also in the extent to which this kind of forward-looking perspective is a matter of concern to them. Mothers probably differed as well in the extent to which they had conscious teaching aims, though, perhaps to please the interviewer, virtually all mothers responded with at least one aim for each activity. Accordingly, we have used caution when reducing interviews and analyzing data. Rather than reporting specific activity level codes, we analyzed only the complexity level of past play relative to current play and of current play relative to prospective play, allowing for considerable error in mothers' estimates, yet retaining information central for understanding the shifting organization of children's numerical activities. In addition, we placed more import on analyses of past to current play, using analyses of current to projected play as corroboration.

METHOD

We provide here an overview of the interview procedure (for the complete procedure, see App. D).

Interview Procedure

In the first interview phase, mothers were asked to describe the organization of current play with the selected easy or difficult activity. (We counterbalanced the order of discussion of the two selected activities within age and social class groups.) Mothers detailed, when possible, their teaching goals for each activity and the amount of guidance they provided for each of their teaching goals on a seven-point scale (1 = low guidance, 7 = high guidance).

In the second phase, mothers were asked to describe play with the activity in the past when it was initially introduced and to project future play. In both cases, mothers again were questioned about teaching goals and guidance.

In the third phase, the relation between the selected activities and other current, past, and projected activities was explored. For each activity, mothers were asked to describe (1) other current activities motivated by the same teaching goals; (2) activities in early play that they believed were preparatory for the selected activity; and (3) projected activities for which the selected activity might be preparatory.

Coding

All activity descriptions and teaching goals were coded using the four-level scale detailed in Chapter V (see Table 15). In addition, shifts in set size and in assistance for teaching goals were coded from past to current and from current to projected play.

Interrater agreement was calculated on 12 randomly selected interviews across age and social class groups. Interrater agreement on codable activities, teaching goals, and set-size shifts was 95% (394 of 416 activities). Of those activities and teaching goals coded by each rater, perfect agreement was achieved on 95% (373 instances). For set-size shifts, out of 394 agreed instances, coders achieved perfect agreement on 94% of the codes (370 instances).

An Example of the Shifting Organization of a Difficult Activity

A condensed sample interview with a middle-class mother of a 4-year-old describing a selected activity, the "Clock Game," provides illustrative examples of our analyses.

The Clock Game.—Clara (the mother) and Annie (her 4-year-old daughter) had been playing the Clock Game for about 18 months and had recently been playing the game about once every 2 weeks. Clara had played the game with her own mother when she was a little girl and now found it to be a game that Annie enjoyed.

As explained by Clara, in the Clock Game a player holds a deck of playing cards. The player turns the cards one at a time and places them in an imaginary clock according to their numerical value (ace = 1, deuce = 2, . . . , jack = 11, queen = 12); all kings are placed in the middle of the clock. On turning up duplicates, the cards are placed on top of their matches. A player "wins" if all four-of-a-kinds are achieved before the four kings are placed in the center.

Shifts in the activity level of the Clock Game.—In current play, the Clock Game was classified as a level 2 activity involving the ordering (or "seriation"), by numerical values, of a single array of elements. Clara generally starts the game for Annie (i.e., begins the initial seriation), and then Annie quickly takes over. In past play—when the game was introduced—the activity had a level 1 goal structure that primarily involved number recognition: not only did Clara start the game for Annie, but also, every time Annie turned a card, Clara asked Annie its number and placed the card for her. For projected play, Clara said that she did not believe that she and Annie would be playing the activity in a fundamentally different way; rather, she expected that Annie would soon be doing the activity completely on her own.

Shifts in the set size of play for the Clock Game.—Though Clara said that she had never varied the highest values of the cards in the past, and though she did not project that she would do so in the future, such variations would be possible, and many mothers in our sample did, in fact, report such set-size shifts in similar games.

Shifts in Clara's teaching goals for the Clock Game.—Clara reported three teaching goals related to current play: (1) to learn to recognize numbers (level 1: number recognition); (2) to understand a succession—that the numbers are ordered (level 2: single-array ordinal representation); and (3) to understand that the number of things on a card (such as hearts, diamonds, or spades) are equal to a number such as "five" (level 2: single-array cardinal representation). Clara explained that, when Annie had difficulty recognizing the numeral on the card, she would ask Annie to count the symbols (i.e., hearts, spades, etc.) and that, when she had difficulty in placing the card in its proper position, Clara would ask Annie what number comes before it. Clara reported that some of her current teaching goals differed from the goals she had when she first introduced the activity—she had abandoned some of her original goals and had adopted new ones. For instance, Clara reported that the concern with cardinality was not a goal when the activity was initially introduced, whereas an initial concern for merely "showing her what the numbers looked like, that one 'two' looked like another 'two,'" was an important goal during early play and then later abandoned when Annie understood it. In her projections for future play, Clara reported that she would soon no longer have number recognition as a teaching goal in the Clock Game (". . . because it only goes up to 10. I can see where we'd have to do something different to make her recognize higher numbers. Chutes and Ladders because that has higher numbers—it goes up to 100"). Clara said she would retain her concern that Annie identify particular number words with single arrays of objects (". . . that's important. That I'll probably work on more because, when she starts learning to add, they have to do that all over again").

Shifts in the extent of Clara's assistance in the Clock Game for specific teaching goals.—For the Clock Game, Clara said that, during past play, she provided Annie with a little help in reading numbers (first current goal) and that she demonstrated the process of ordering the cards (second current goal): "I would have to tell her. She'd usually recognize the numbers, but we'd say which number would come first, seven or eight? I'd start one, two, three, four, five, six, seven, and she'd say, 'Yeah, seven before eight.'" When asked to anticipate the amount of assistance she would be providing in the future, Clara responded that she believed that she would be providing no assistance in numeral recognition (first current goal) and less assistance on helping Annie order the cards (second current goal) but that she anticipated providing more assistance for relating the numerals on the playing cards to their values (third current goal): "I'll probably work on that more because, when she starts learning to add, they have to do that all over again. . . . That's something I should keep going over with her."

The relation of the Clock Game to other current, past, and projected numerical activities.—It was also clear in Clara's interview that the Clock Game was one activity in a large matrix of activities that displayed similarities and differences to the Clock Game.

For current play, Clara made it clear that her current teaching goals for the Clock Game often cut across different activities. For each Clock Game goal, Clara described other current activities she played with Annie in which she had the same goal. For instance, for the goal of ordering a set of elements with respect to their numerical values (level 2), Clara reported that she and Annie talk about the age relation of Annie to her younger and older brothers, and Clara helps Annie locate a television channel between two others (channel 4 comes after channel 2 and before channel 5).

For past play, Clara cited a number of activities she believed were preparatory for the Clock Game. Clara cited the game "Concentration with Playing Cards" (level 1) as an early activity in which Annie got "used to seeing numbers a lot." Clara also said that, "as for matching the numbers [in the Clock Game], she had to know what they looked like through the other activities . . . [such as] TV and books."

Clara cited a number of possible future activities (projected) for which the Clock Game might be preparatory. Chutes and Ladders, a game that contains numbers up to 100, was one possibility: "I'd like her to master that a little bit. She has trouble with that because the numbers go so high. I'd like her to learn higher numbers" (level 1, numeral recognition, increase in set size), writing numbers on her own, and adding numbers (level 4).

RESULTS

We organize our results with respect to discontinuities in the goal structure organization of play over time and note the continuities of play in the context of these discontinuities. In our analyses, we pooled age and social class groups since preliminary chi-square analyses yielded no differences as

a function of these variables. First we present analyses of the activities selected by the mothers, and then we present analyses of activities related to
the selected activities.

Analyses of Selected Activities

Shifts in the goal structure complexity of activities.—Shifts over time in the
goal structure complexity of play were analyzed for both the easy and the
difficult activities for shifts from past to current play and from current to
projected play. For each analysis, we assigned dyads to one of three direction
of shift categories: (1) the down shift category consisted of changes to less
complex goal structures; (2) the unchanged category consisted of no change
in goal structure complexity; and (3) the up shift category consisted of a
change to a more complex goal structure (including shifts from a demonstration to interactive play).

Table 42 contains the percentage of mothers classified into each shift
category for past to current play and for current to projected play. The
majority of mothers tended not to describe shifts in the goal structure of
children's activities, though, when they did, they tended to describe shifts to
higher-level activity structures (past to current, easy: $\chi^2[1, N = 19] = 15.2$,
$p < .001$; difficult: $\chi^2[1, N = 14] = 10.29$, $p < .01$; current to projected,
easy: $\chi^2[1, N = 13] = 1.92$, $p =$ N.S.; difficult: $\chi^2[1, N = 19] = 4.26$, $p <$
.05). Of those mothers who did not describe subsequent play at higher
levels, many did, however, describe subsequent play as shifting to greater
set-size values: of those mothers who did not shift the goal structure of play
to higher levels, 39% and 40% described current play at greater set-size
levels than prior play on the easy and difficult activities, respectively, and

TABLE 42

PERCENT DISTRIBUTION OF MOTHERS REPORTING COMPLEXITY-LEVEL SHIFTS IN THE
GOAL STRUCTURE OF PLAY OVER TIME

TIME PERIOD	DIRECTION OF SHIFT		
	Down	Unchanged	Up
Easy activity:			
Past to current (74)	1	75	24 [4]
Current to projected (76)	5	83	10
Difficult activity:			
Past to current (72)	1	80 [8]	18
Current to projected (71)	7	73	20

NOTE.—Numbers in parentheses represent sample sizes; numbers in square brackets indicate percent of dyads who
shifted from a maternal demonstration of the activity to interaction.

30% and 56% described projected play at greater set-size levels than current play on the easy and difficult activities, respectively. In fact, there is evidence that there was a trade-off between shifts to greater complexity levels and shifts to greater levels of set size: mothers who did not describe upward shifts in the goal structure complexity of play described set-size shifts to greater levels more frequently than did mothers who described upward shifts in the goal structure complexity of play (past to current, easy: $\chi^2[1, N = 24] = 10.67, p < .001$; difficult: $\chi^2[1, N = 23] = 15.70, p < .001$; current to projected, easy: $\chi^2[1, N = 21] = 17.19, p < .001$; difficult: $\chi^2[1, N = 32] = 32.0, p < .001$). A small proportion of mothers reported that they shifted simultaneously to lower levels of set size and greater activity complexity levels (or to greater levels of set size and lower levels of activity complexity), coordinated shifts that accentuate the trade-off between these two aspects of activity organization.

Shifts in teaching goals.—Maternal teaching goals are a second index of the goal structure complexity of play. Many mothers reported more than one teaching goal for each current activity: 44% of mothers for the easy activity and 66% for the difficult activity.

As children acquire greater competence, mothers may abandon goals and introduce new ones in the same nominal activity. Table 43 contains the percentage of mothers who cited at least one goal in past play that was not a goal in current play (abandoned past), at least one current goal projected not to be a future goal (abandoned current), at least one current goal that was not an initial goal (novel current), and at least one projected goal that was not a current goal (novel projected). Mothers' teaching goals were frequently abandoned and new ones generated in the context of the same activity. To determine the relation between abandoned, current, and novel projected teaching goals, the mean goal level for each was calculated. Dyads were then assigned to one of three categories: (1) down shift included mothers who had lower mean goal levels for current relative to past play or for projected relative to current play; (2) unchanged included mothers with

TABLE 43

PERCENTAGES OF MOTHERS WHO CITED ABANDONED AND NOVEL GOALS OVER PAST TO
CURRENT AND CURRENT TO PROJECTED PLAY FOR EASY AND DIFFICULT ACTIVITIES

ACTIVITY TYPE	STATUS OF MOTHERS' GOALS							
	Abandoned Past		Abandoned Current		Novel Current		Novel Projected	
	%	N	%	N	%	N	%	N
Easy	38	78	58	74	43	76	38	78
Difficult	41	78	52	74	40	73	33	78

no difference in mean goal levels over the respective time periods; and (3) up shift included mothers who had higher goal levels over the respective time periods.

Table 44 contains a cross-tabulation of shifts in teaching-goal indices for abandoned, current, and novel projected goals. Mothers reported shifts in teaching goals to higher levels of complexity for only one of the four shift types (for current to novel projected for the easy activity, $\chi^2[1, N = 27] = 6.26, p < .05$). However, mothers who shifted to a lower index or who did not shift in index level often reported shifts to higher levels of set size (abandoned to current, easy: 65%; difficult: 67%; current to novel projected, easy: 86%; difficult: 61%). Moreover, for mothers whose teaching goals remained constant over time, mothers frequently reported providing or projected that they would provide less assistance (past to current, easy: 81%; difficult: 59%; current to projected, easy: 57%; difficult: 52%).

Analyses of Related Activities

Just as there are continuous and discontinuous features of a single activity over time in social interactions, there are discontinuous and continuous features between a selected activity and (a) other current activities, (b) past activities that may have been preparatory for the selected activities, and (c) projected activities for which the selected activities may be preparatory. Our final analyses document continuities and discontinuities between the targeted activities and current, past, and projected activities.

Table 45 contains the percent of mothers who reported other activities in current play for which they had the same teaching goals as the selected activities. These percentages range from 65% to 100%, indicating that most children participate with multiple activities for which mothers have similar, if not identical, teaching goals.

TABLE 44

PERCENTAGE OF COMPLEXITY-LEVEL SHIFTS CONTRASTING ABANDONED WITH CURRENT
AND CURRENT WITH NOVEL PROJECTED GOALS

	DIRECTION OF SHIFT		
TYPE OF GOAL SHIFT	Down	Unchanged	Up
Easy activity:			
Abandoned to current goals (29)	28	31	41
Current to novel projected goals (49)	14	45	40
Difficult activity:			
Abandoned to current goals (29)	31	42	27
Current to novel projected goals (50)	14	40	46

NOTE.—Numbers in parentheses represent sample sizes.

TABLE 45

PERCENTAGE OF MOTHERS WHO CITED MORE THAN ONE ACTIVITY FOR
ANY STATED TEACHING GOAL

| | EASY ACTIVITY | | DIFFICULT ACTIVITY | |
GROUP	%	N	%	N
Middle class:				
2-year-olds	100	20	85	20
4-year-olds	75	20	70	20
Working class:				
2-year-olds	100	18	100	18
4-year-olds	70	20	65	20

To analyze maternal reports of past and projected activities, activities that mothers believed were preparatory for the selected activities and for which the selected activities were preparatory were coded for goal complexity level. For each analysis, dyads were assigned to one of three categories: (1) down shift included mothers who reported shifts over time to a lower level of goal structure complexity; (2) unchanged included mothers who reported no shift in goal structure complexity level; and (3) up shift included those mothers who reported a shift to a higher goal structure complexity level.

Table 46 contains the results of our analyses. Mothers frequently reported activities with lower goal structure complexity levels as precursors to future activities. However, the likelihood that mothers would report activities at lower as opposed to higher complexity levels as preparatory activities achieved statistical significance only for the preparatory to current activities

TABLE 46

PERCENTAGE OF COMPLEXITY-LEVEL SHIFTS CONTRASTING ACTIVITIES MOTHERS CITED AS
PREPARATORY FOR SELECTED ACTIVITY AND ACTIVITIES MOTHERS PROJECTED WILL
BUILD ON SELECTED ACTIVITY

| | DIRECTION OF SHIFT | | |
TYPE OF SHIFT	Down	Unchanged	Up
Easy activity:			
Past activities as preparatory for selected activity	14	8	78
Projected activities as building on selected activity	37	9	54
Difficult activity:			
Past activities as preparatory for selected activities	23	10	66
Projected activities as building on selected activity	38	17	45

NOTE.—$N = 78$.

(contrasting down shift to up shift, easy: $\chi^2[1, N = 72] = 34.72, p < .001$; difficult: $\chi^2[1, N = 70] = 16.51, p < .001$).

SUMMARY AND DISCUSSION

The findings in this chapter point to continuous and discontinuous features in the social organization of children's numerical activities over the course of their early development. Discontinuities include shifts in the goal structure of play (activity-level shifts) and qualitative shifts in mothers' teaching goals (abandoning goals and adopting new ones). We found that, over time, mothers shifted the goal structure complexity of play in the selected activities, their teaching goals in the selected activities, and the goal complexity structure of current and projected relative to preparatory activities. When mothers did not report shifts coded at higher complexity levels, they reported quantitative decreases in maternal assistance and/or increases in the set size of play.

Through the interweaving of continuous and discontinuous features of number activities over time, novel problem contexts emerge for children that are related to their past accomplishments. We pointed to many regularities in our data that were illustrative of this mesh. For instance, the reduction in set size as a mother first assists her child count a single array of seven beads and then transforms the game into a comparison activity (three beads vs. five) enables the child to make use of previous accomplishments when identifying new numerical functions of number words. Similarly, the increase in set size in a single-array counting activity provides a context in which a child might extend his or her ability to achieve single-array goals through the elaboration of new strategies to keep track of which objects have and have not been counted. Thus, just as children's number development can be understood in terms of shifting relations between form and function, the social organization of young children's numerical activities can be understood as providing opportunities for children both to use their previous accomplishments to serve new functions and to elaborate and increasingly specialize their existing strategies.

IX. SOCIAL AND DEVELOPMENTAL PROCESSES IN CHILDREN'S UNDERSTANDING OF NUMBER

Any model that addresses the role of social factors in cognitive development must contain an analysis of the character of children's socially organized experience and its relation to cognitive-developmental processes. Previous models, whether they have been "socialization" accounts (e.g., Bernstein, 1972; Hess & Shipman, 1965; Marjoribanks, 1979), developmental-constructivist accounts (e.g., Dasen, 1972, 1980; Piaget, 1966), or the recent neo-Vygotskiian writings (e.g., Rogoff et al., 1984; Wertsch, 1979, 1985, 1986), have not provided adequate accounts of the interplay between the child's developing understandings and sociocultural processes. In this concluding chapter, we review the problems with previous accounts and the contribution of our own work.

SOME PROBLEMS WITH PREVIOUS ACCOUNTS OF CHILDREN'S SOCIALLY ORGANIZED EXPERIENCE

In socialization models, children's socially organized experience—to the extent that it is addressed at all—is defined either by aspects of maternal behavior such as mothers' praise, punitiveness, and provision of appropriate play materials or by general indices of maternal behavior such as mothers' education, values, and aspirations for their children. Such social variables are then related to children's cognitive abilities. Though results from this literature have shown that such social variables are often related to children's progress in acquiring cognitive skills, the analysis of the maternal role in the nature of children's experience remains inadequate in two ways. First, since socialization models do not provide analyses of children's roles in conceptualizing and generating the socially organized tasks with which they interact, there is little basis for understanding whether and/or in what way codified dimensions of maternal behavior are penetrating children's ongoing construal of tasks. Second, the concern with factors external to the child also precludes analyses of the dynamic character of the environments that emerge in social interactions, environments in which the activity of the adult is guided by and is also a guide to the behavior and understandings of the child. Lacking a coordinated analysis of the joint production of socially organized experience by both mother and child, socialization accounts can make little headway in producing substantive treatments of the interplay between social and developmental processes in children's understandings.

Developmental-constructivist accounts (e.g., Piaget, 1970; Werner & Kaplan, 1963) and some recent information-processing formulations (e.g., Greeno et al., 1984) do focus on children's understandings and goal-directed activities as pivotal constructs. These accounts typically offer analyses of formalized cognitive structures, and children's goal-directed activities are one manifestation of these structures. While such accounts have contributed substantially to our knowledge of children's developing understandings, strategies, and skills, still missing are analyses of the cultural activities in which children's cognitive activities are embedded and an account of how the organization of these activities, jointly produced by children and adults, provides a context in which cultural achievements are interwoven with children's developing cognitions.

Within the Vygotsky-inspired research, there is an examination of aspects of the social organization of children's experience with goal-directed activities. The approach is based on the assumption that the characteristics of adult-guided interactions are interiorized by the young child in development and that the interiorizations come to constitute the conscious problem-solving activities of the older child. This theoretical posture has led researchers to produce analyses of the social organization of adult-child teaching interactions with children of different age levels. Though Vygotsky-inspired analyses have demonstrated that adults' involvement in children's solutions to tasks diminishes with children's age and that children gradually initiate problem-solving strategies previously directed by adults, generally lacking in Vygotsky-inspired treatments are substantive analyses of developmental shifts in children's goal-directed activities and a cultural analysis of children's participation in activity structures. As a consequence, though we have in this literature evidence of the changing organization of children's socially organized experience, the descriptions produced have provided no clear formulation of how the child transforms cultural forms into his or her own developing conceptual understanding.

THE INTERPLAY BETWEEN SOCIAL AND DEVELOPMENTAL PROCESSES

The concern of the research approach developed in this *Monograph* has been to provide an integrated framework for analyzing social and developmental processes in children's numerical understandings. In our treatment, children's numerical achievements are understood as their goal-directed adaptations to their environments—environments generated through their participation in sociocultural activities. Such generated environments constitute children's socially organized experience. A description of socially organized experience necessarily depends on our three analytic components: (1) a developmental analysis of form-function shifts in children's goal-directed activities involving number, (2) a cultural analysis of the shifting activities in which such shifts are embedded, and (3) a social interactional analysis of the way ongoing form-function shifts in children's developing numerical cognitions are facilitated by and interwoven with cultural activities in adult-child interactions.

The Dynamics of Form-Function Relations in Children's Developing Numerical Cognitions

Children's capability to generate numerical goals both enables and constrains their construal of and participation in social activities involving number. A developmental analysis of shifts in children's goal-directed activities—the first of our three analytic components—is therefore critical for understanding developmental shifts in the character of children's numerical achievements and for understanding the nature of children's numerical environments generated during social activities.

We have argued that early number development can be understood as shifting relations between numerical forms and numerical functions. Our analyses of children's numerical understandings revealed evidence of such shifts between 2 and 4 years of age across virtually our entire battery of assessment tasks. We illustrate the nature of form-function shifts with two task types—complex counting and number reproduction, activities with level 2 and 3 goal structures, respectively (on the basis of our four-level scheme; see Table 15).

On the complex counting task, we found evidence that, early in development, young children often use number word forms to serve the function of nominal enumerations (level 1). In the set 5 and 13 tasks, younger children often assigned number words to the arrays by global sweeping and/or global pulsing gestures. The lack of concern for one-to-one correspondences in these forms of number word assignments indicates that younger children were denoting, with number words, either individual elements in an array, segments of the array, or the entire array. Typically, children using this nominal enumerative function also used idiosyncratic number word sequence forms, forms well suited for nominal enumerations but not for number representation and communication about number. Analysis of the set 13 task produced evidence of a shift to a numerical representation function (level 2) of number words. However, the strategic forms that less sophisticated children used were still clumsy and ill suited to problems that are generated in counting a large set—such as children's proximal strategies. More advanced children—primarily the 4-year-olds—made systematic efforts to assign number words in a one-to-one correspondence using more specialized peripheral or linear strategies, forms better suited for dealing with the problems of counting large sets. The more advanced children were also more likely to count with standard number word forms, forms better suited for communication about and representation of number.

Evidence of form-function shifts was also reported in the analyses of children's solution strategies for the number reproduction task. Young children tended not to treat the tasks as ones requiring an exact numerical reproduction (level 3) or even a numerical representation (level 2)—they merely retrieved some or all of the pennies from an available set to produce a copy of the model set. Analyses of set 9 revealed that older, more advanced children attempted to accomplish a single-array representation (level 2) in their solution to the tasks. To do this, they applied their previously acquired number word forms to serve the newly emerging single-array function of producing a count of the copy and/or the model. However, they did not use the information produced by the count to achieve a numerical reproduction (level 3). Older children deployed the forms generated for single-array counts to serve a newly emerging numerical reproduction function. They produced multiple single-array counts and, through trial-and-error additions/subtractions and recounts, tried to equalize the model and the copy. Gradually, children generate systematic procedures to reproduce the model array.

Children's Engagement with Cultural Activities Involving Number

As children's ability to produce numerical goals of different complexity levels changes with development, so do the goal structures of the sociocultural activities involving number that are an impetus for children's construction of goals. Indeed, we expected that progress in one enables progress in the other. An analysis of children's participation with and the structure of sociocultural number activities is our second analytic component.

Our interviews with mothers revealed that, across our age and social class groups, children regularly participated in activities involving number, activities that did have goal structures of varying levels of complexity. Such activities included games of the dyads' own invention (e.g., counting stairs), store-bought games (e.g., dominoes), and number books (books designed to teach children about number). The high level of frequency of games of dyads' own invention across social class groups makes clear the everyday character of number play in both groups. As expected, we found age differences in the goal structure complexity of home activities, differences that mirrored our developmental analyses of children's achievements: younger children, children who showed competence reflecting level 1 goals, tended to be engaged with activities of level 1 and 2 goal structures; older children, children who showed competence reflecting higher-level goals, tended to be engaged with activities with higher-level goal structures. Working-class 4-year-olds tended to be engaged with social activities of less complex goal structure than were their middle-class peers, again reflecting social class differences in children's numerical achievements. Thus, the structure of children's everyday activities and their numerical understandings mesh with one another, a relation that supports our claim for their reciprocal dependence.

The Emergent Organization of Numerical Activities in Mother-Child Interactions

Children's goals constructed in the course of mother-child interactions emerge through a negotiated process between children and their mothers, one in which mothers adjust the organization of tasks to their children's efforts to accomplish activity-related goals and in which children adjust their goal-directed activities to their mothers' efforts at guidance.

To examine the negotiated organization of cultural activities in adult-child interactions, we observed mother-child play with the complex counting and number reproduction activities. In our analysis, we intended to capture the interplay between children's production of goals and means to achieve them and mothers' contributions to the organization of children's numerical activities. There were three consistent patterns of findings across the activities.

First, during the interactions, mothers adjusted the goal structure of the tasks to their children's abilities. Mothers of less able children were more likely to use instructions that transformed each task to a more elementary goal structure. The complex counting activity (level 2) had the character of a level 1 activity whenever a mother was primarily concerned with instructing her child in the conventional sequence of number words rather than in the numerical representation of the entire target set. Similarly, the number reproduction activity (level 3) had the character of a level 2 activity whenever mothers focused on eliciting from the child a numerical representation of single sets (level 2) without explaining the numerical reproduction goal, and it had the character of a level 1 activity whenever mothers focused assistance just on application of number words to individual objects. Mothers' instructions also varied as a function of the set size of the array—again reflecting maternal adjustments to children's greater difficulty with the conditions of the larger set: within dyads, instructions during the larger-set-size conditions emerged at less sophisticated goal complexity levels than did those that emerged during the smaller-set-size conditions.

Second, mothers adjusted the goal structure of the task to children's successes and difficulties during the activity. In the complex counting task, when children made either a number word sequence error or a one-to-one correspondence error, mothers adjusted the content of their assistance to the type of error the child produced and, following either type of error, shifted the organization of the task to a more elementary level of goal structure and/or offered more specified assistance. In the number reproduction activity, mothers shifted to more superordinate levels of task organization following children's accurate counts and shifted to more subordinate levels following inaccurate counts. For both tasks, in each analysis of maternal shift, there were no effects for age, set size, or social class, a pattern of findings indicating that ongoing maternal adjustments to success and failure are stable characteristics of mother-child teaching interactions.

Third, children often adjusted their performance to their mothers' goal-related directives. In the complex counting activities, the majority of children shifted their ongoing behavior as they attempted to accomplish the goals specified in their mothers' correspondence and sequence directives. In the number reproduction activity, children who did not appropriately count one or both sets when unassisted (an important strategic component in the solution of the task) were likely to count with their mothers' assistance. In both activities, children who did not successfully complete the task on their own were likely to do so with their mothers.

These patterns of maternal and child adjustments show that mothers are adjusting their goal-related directives to their children's understandings and task-related accomplishments and that children are adjusting their goal-directed activities to their mothers' efforts to organize the task. Thus, children's socially organized experiences with number in everyday number activities are emergent ones; they are not "contained in" social practices or in the minds of the participants but are negotiated in interactions and emerge as a result of the mothers' and children's adjusted efforts to accomplish numerical tasks jointly.

The Shifting Organization of Social Interactions Involving Number over Children's Early Development

The three analytic components reviewed above demonstrate the contribution of the child and the mother in generating socially organized experience linked to children's developing understandings. We have yet to consider, however, how the organization of social experience shifts over individual children's early development and the interplay between this shifting organization and shifts in children's understandings.

The longitudinal portrayals of the shifting organization of dyadic play in everyday activities (Chap. VIII) provided insight into the continuities and discontinuities over time in the social organization of children's everyday number activities. Discontinuities were documented in shifts in the goal complexity levels of number activities and maternal teaching goals for number activities, shifts that create contexts for children to generate novel numerical functions. Thus, a mother might shift in focus from counting objects in a marble game to comparing subsets of marbles, shifting the organization of play from a focus on single-array number representations (level 2) to one on numerical comparisons (level 3). Such shifts provide the child with opportunities to extend previously acquired strategic forms to newly emerging numerical functions. Often, when mothers did not report discontinuous shifts, they reported shifts that preserved the goal structure level of the activity but required children to elaborate further their means of accomplishing the goals of the activity. Thus, mothers reported increasing over time the set size of play or decreasing the amount of assistance they provided for the same teaching goals in play. Such continuities provide opportunities for a child further to specialize forms to accomplish preexisting functions. Thus, the continuities and discontinuities in the organization of play are the social complement of form-function shifts in children's developing understandings. Through the interweaving of continuities and discontinuities in the organization of number play over time, children generate novel functions in using their previously acquired forms and generate new, more specialized forms to serve preexisting functions.

Social Class and Early Number Development

We included social class as a variable, considering it as a gross index of cultural practices involving number. Social class differences in children's cognitive achievements have been examined frequently in previous research motivated by socialization accounts. However, we intended to produce an alternative account of social class influences, one grounded in our three-component approach.

In our study, children of both social class groups elaborated goals of varying levels of complexity (developmental component), were engaged with cultural number activities of varying levels of complexity (sociocultural component), and contributed, in interactions with their mothers, to emergent number environments in which mothers and children adjusted to one another's efforts to accomplish the task (social interactional component). However, there was an integrated pattern of social class differences across our three components. For the developmental component, we found that working-class children's numerical achievements on the unassisted tasks (primarily on tasks with more complex goal structures) were lower than were those of their middle-class peers. For the sociocultural component, we found that working-class mothers expected that their children would not complete an equivalent number of years of schooling or attain the same level of employment as their middle-class peers and that working-class mothers of 4-year-olds expressed slightly less interest in their children's number activities than did middle-class mothers of 4-year-olds. More important, working-class 4-year-olds were engaged at home with number activities of less complex goal structures than were their middle-class peers. Finally, for the social-interactional component, we found that working-class mothers structured the number reproduction task and the set 13 complex counting task at lower levels of goal complexity than did their middle-class peers. This configuration of social class differences in children's achievements, home activities, and maternal values and in the emergent goal structure of mother-child interactions is one that we expected to find. Dyads in the different social class groups were creating somewhat different environments in their everyday lives, but, for each group, the process of creating those environments is the same: through children's participation in socially organized activities, children are both influencing and influenced by the goal structure of these activities, and, in attempting to conceptualize and achieve those goals, children generate novel numerical understandings.

CONCLUDING REMARKS

The construct of socially organized experience is critical in any account of cognitive development insofar as it constitutes the "material" out of which children produce novel cognitive developments. We have noted that past analyses have tended either to disregard the child's role as a participant in generating social experience or to neglect the role of social practices as an organizational impetus for the child's social experience. In our work, we have shown that children's numerical goals and the goal structure of social practices become linked in children's everyday number activities. Children re-create the goal structure of social activities on their own terms, injecting their own means of solution while at the same time adjusting and negotiating the structure of activities with adults. Numerical environments are thus constituted through this process of active participation and negotiation. By generating new goals and means of achieving them in adult-guided activities, children generate further understandings—understandings necessarily linked both to social life and to their own constructive efforts.

INTERVIEW PROCEDURE FOR MOTHERS' REPORTS OF HOME NUMBER ACTIVITIES

INTERVIEW

To allow them some time to reflect about the character of their number play prior to our face-to-face interview, mothers were mailed a brief questionnaire. The interviewer then used the mother's written response to this questionnaire as a basis to begin the interview.

The interview was partitioned into phases: an introduction, mothers' description of each type of activity the dyad used, mothers' rankings of these activities with respect to their relative frequency of use and perceived importance for teaching about number, and mothers' evaluations of their own and their children's interest in the elicited number activities. The interview lasted about half an hour. All interviews were administered by a single member of the research staff and were audiotaped for later coding.

Introduction

As you know, we're interested in how young children learn about numbers and counting at home. I'd like to ask you some questions about the sorts of games and activities [child's name] might be doing at home in the past few months that you think may help him/her learn about numbers. I'll be asking you about games, books, puzzles, toys, games of your own invention, activities—anything you can think of—that may help to teach numbers, counting, and maybe even addition and subtraction. Also, if you can think of other things that just use numbers but may not be intended to really teach, let me know. OK?

Store-bought Games

First, I'd like to talk with you about some of the store-bought games and puzzles [child's name] has. You've listed several here [on preliminary questionnaire], and I would like to go through them with you, one at a time. [For each one listed, the following questions were asked.] Could you describe it for me? How do you and [child's name] use the game? In particular, what do you do and what does [child's name] do? [The interviewer continued probing until he had a clear description of the character of the interaction. The interviewer recorded the name of each game on a separate card for later use and then probed for other games and activities. The interview then continued as follows.] Some of these games may be specifically intended to teach about numbers, while some others may just involve numbers or counting but are not meant to teach. Could you tell me which ones you think are meant to teach about numbers and which just use numbers? [On the basis of the mother's response, the interviewer constructed two piles with the cards, one for games specifically intended for teaching and the other for games that used numbers but were not specifically intended for teaching.]

Teaching Games

Of these games that are intended to teach about numbers, about how often does [child's name] play with any of these at home? (a) once a month, (b) twice a month, (c) once a week, (d) twice a week, (e) four or five times a week, or (f) every day? I'd like you to take these cards [games intended to teach] and order them from those [child's name] plays most often to those he/she plays the least. Now I'd like you to take the same cards and order them from the ones you think are the most important for teaching and learning about number concepts to those you think are the least important.

Games That Use Numbers

[The identical procedures were used to elicit descriptions of non-teaching activities that use numbers.]

Number Books

Now I'd like to ask you about books. You've listed several books that [child's name] has. [If no number books were listed, the interviewer asked if the mother used any number books with her child.] Could you describe them? [The interviewer proceeded through the mother's list of number books, asking for a description of each and how they are read. Once the list was completed, the interviewer asked if there were any additional number books. If the mother cited any number books, the interviewer asked,] About how often does [child's name] look at any books that involve numbers or counting? (a) once a month, (b) twice a month, (c) once a week, (d) twice a week, (e) four or five times a week, or (f) every day?

Games of Own Invention

You've also listed some things that you and [child's name] do together in day-to-day activities that involve numbers or counting. [If none was listed, the interviewer asked if there were any games of their own invention involving numbers that the mother and child played, and he gave as examples counting steps or setting the table. For each activity, the interviewer elicited a description.] How often does [child's name] do any of these activities or games of your own invention that involve numbers or counting? (a) once a month, (b) twice a month, (c) once a week, (d) twice a week, (e) four or five times a week, or (f) everyday? Now, I'd like you to put these in order from the ones you think [child's name] learns the most about numbers from to the ones you think he/she learns the least about numbers from.

Mothers' and Children's Interest in Number Activities

You've listed a few times when [child's name] seems to use numbers or counts spontaneously without your encouragement. Would you describe these? How often does [child's name] seem to count spontaneously? (a) once a month, (b) twice a month, (c) once a week, (d) twice a week, (e) four or five times a week, or (f) everyday? In the past few months, how interested has [child's name] been in numbers or counting? [The mother was presented with a seven-point scale from "not very interested at all" to "extremely interested."] How would you characterize your interest and involvement in doing number or counting activities with [child's name] in the last few months? [The mother was presented with a seven-point scale from "not very interested at all" to "extremely interested."]

CODING SCHEME FOR ACTIVITY LEVELS AND MATERNAL TEACHING GOALS (FOR CHAPTERS V AND VIII)

LEVEL 1

Nonnumerical activities that involved number words or numerals were coded as level 1. These include rote counting activities such as numeral recitations, numeral recognition activities (e.g., a mother may point to a plastic numeral and ask, "What number is this?"), and numeral matching activities (e.g., a mother may point to a plastic numeral and ask the child to find the same written numeral).

LEVEL 2

Activities that involved the cardinal and/or ordinal representations of single arrays were coded as level 2. These include object counting (e.g., a mother may refer to a group of objects and ask the child, "Count these"), cardinal questions (e.g., "How many are there?"), activities involving the production of a specified numerical value (e.g., "Get five pennies from that pile"), relating written number symbols to sets (e.g., showing the child a written numeral and asking the child to get the same number of pennies), and counting different sets of objects showing that anything can be counted.

LEVEL 3

Activities that involved the cardinal and/or ordinal representations and comparisons of two or more arrays were coded as level 3. These include ordinal comparisons of any two values with respect to which number is prior to another (e.g., "Which number is first, one or two?"), cardinal comparisons of any two values with respect to their equivalence or nonequivalence (including establishing one-to-one correspondences between sets to serve this end), ordinal correspondences such as seriating a set of ordinal values, and activities organized to teach commutative and associative equivalencies between sets.

LEVEL 4

Activities that involved the composition or decomposition of numerical values through arithmetic operations were coded as level 4 activities. These include all arithmetic activities (e.g., addition and subtraction) with or without objects present and activities concerned with teaching base structure conventions.

ACTIVITIES CODED AS MISCELLANEOUS

Several activities that did not occur with high frequency were coded as miscellaneous and were not included in our coding hierarchy. These included writing numerals and television shows. Though writing numerals could be considered a level 1 activity, the sensorimotor skills involved made this activity inappropriate for our analytic scheme. Television shows were not included since we did not have enough information to code these shows with respect to our scheme.

ANALYSES OF THE MODEL-SET AND AVAILABLE-SET PHASES ON THE NUMBER REPRODUCTION TASK FOR EXCLUDED DYADS

MOTHERS' INSTRUCTION DURING SIMPLIFIED AND/OR UNSUCCESSFUL MODEL-SET PHASES

The Pearson correlations reported in Table 37 were repeated for subjects excluded either because mothers had simplified the task in the model-set phase or because the dyad had been unsuccessful in accomplishing a representation of the model set, or both. (Mothers' last instruction in the model-set phase was not examined here because it was intended as a measure of mothers' means of assisting children through the transition from a successful model-set phase, at whatever level of assistance, to the available-set phase.) Table C1 contains, for the excluded subjects, the correlations, for each set size, of mothers' instruction with children's unassisted performance, age, and social class. There were few subjects for both sets, particularly for median level of mothers' instruction.

There were two significant correlations. In set 3, mothers (of excluded subjects) were less likely to explain the superordinate goal to children of greater ability, a relation opposite to that found for dyads who were successful in set 3 (Table 37). A possible interpretation of this pattern is that inadequate maternal instruction contributed to failure on set 3. In set 9, mothers provided less specified instruction to children of greater ability, a relation parallel to the relation between instruction and child's ability for successful dyads.

TABLE C1

Pearson Correlation Coefficients for Maternal Instruction in Unsuccessful and/or Simplified Model-Set Phases with Children's Unassisted Performance, Age, and Social Class

Mothers' Instruction	Unassisted Performance	Age	SES	SES. Unassisted Peformance, Age[a]
Set 3:				
Median level (6)	.40	.42	−.08	.12
Most specified (11)	.05	.15	−.45	−.42
Superordinate (11)	−.52*	−.36	.21	.13
Set 9:				
Median level (8)	−.32	−.76*	.12	−.46
Most specified (17)	−.16	−.16	.21	.18
Superordinate (17)	−.02	−.07	−.07	−.11

Note.—Numbers in parentheses represent sample sizes.

[a] The correlation between measures of maternal instruction and social class, controlling for unassisted performance and age group.

* $p < .05$.

MOTHERS' INSTRUCTION DURING SIMPLIFIED AND/OR UNSUCCESSFUL AVAILABLE-SET PHASES

The Pearson correlations reported in Table 40 were repeated for subjects excluded either because mothers had simplified the task in the model-set or available-set phases or because the dyad had been unsuccessful in accomplishing a representation of the model set in the available-set phase, or both. Table C2 contains, for the excluded subjects, the correlations, for

TABLE C2

Pearson Correlation Coefficients for Maternal Instruction in Unsuccessful and/or Simplified Available-Set Phases with Children's Unassisted Performance, Age, and Social Class

Mothers' Instruction	Unassisted Performance	Age	SES	SES. Unassisted Peformance, Age[a]
Set 3:				
Median level (28)	−.14	−.33*	−.20	−.36*
Most specified (28)	.12	−.16	−.30†	−.39*
Set 9:				
Median level (42)	−.13	−.05	−.05	−.05
Most specified (42)	−.09	−.08	−.14	−.14

Note.—Numbers in parentheses represent sample sizes.

[a] The correlation between measures of maternal instruction and social class, controlling for unassisted performance and age group.

* $p < .05$.

† $p = .058$.

each set size, of mothers' instruction with children's unassisted performance, age, and social class.

In set 3, mothers of older children provided less specified instruction than did mothers of younger children, a finding parallel to that in Table 40 for successful dyads. Also in set 3, working-class mothers provided more specified instruction than did middle-class mothers, a finding parallel to the relation between SES and instruction found in set 9 for successful dyads.

INTERVIEW PROCEDURE FOR MOTHERS' LONGITUDINAL PORTRAYALS OF EASY AND DIFFICULT ACTIVITIES

The interview described below was administered twice to all mothers, once for an activity that the mothers thought was difficult for their children and once for an activity that the mothers thought was easy. The order of these interviews was counterbalanced within each age and social class group. Mothers were told at the prior session that we would be discussing such activities in the current session to give them an opportunity to reflect about appropriate activities for selection.

Introduction

I'd like you to think back about all the activities from which [child's name] learns about numbers or counting that we discussed in our previous session. I'm going to ask you to think of a hard activity for [child's name] and an easy activity for [child's name]. These should be activities in which you teach [child's name] something about numbers. What's an easy/difficult activity or game that you do involving numbers with [child's name]? [If a mother had difficulty making this distinction, the interviewer told her that any kind of activity would do and provided her with some examples from her previous interview on home activities.]

Current Play

Description of Current Play and Amount of
Involvement with Activity

What happens during the activity? What do you do and what does [child's name] do? [The interviewer tried to elicit a "blueprint" of the organization of the activity.] How long ago did you begin doing this activity with [child's name]? About how often do you play this activity with [child's name]? (*a*) once a month, (*b*) twice a month, (*c*) once a week, (*d*) twice a week, (*e*) four or five times a week, or (*f*) everyday?

Mother's Current Goals and Amount of Assistance

What would you like [child's name] to learn about numbers from this activity? [The interviewer wrote up to four goals on a piece of paper for subsequent reference.] One of the things you want [child's name] to learn about numbers from this activity is [first current goal]. I want you to look at this chart. If you had to give a number between one and seven, and one stands for giving [child's name] little help, and seven stands for giving [child's name] a lot of help, how much help would you say you give [child's name] for learning about [first current goal]? Why this number? [This line of questioning was completed for each of the mother's stated goals.]

Past Play

Description of Past Play with Activity

When you first started this activity *x* months ago [the interviewer used the same number of months the mother offered earlier], did you play it any differently than you do now? Please explain. [The interviewer used follow-up questions to get a clear picture of how the play differed.]

Mother's Past Goals and Amount of Past Assistance

You told me that one of the things you want [child's name] to learn from this activity is [first current goal]. Did you want [child's name] to learn about [first current goal] when you first started the game *x* months ago? [If not,] Why not? [If yes,] I want you to look at this chart. If you had to give a number between one and seven, and one stands for giving [child's name] little help, and seven stands for giving [child's name] a lot of help, how much help would you say you gave [child's name] for learning about [first current goal] when you first started the game *x* months ago? Why this number? [This line of questioning was completed for each of the mother's stated goals.] You've told me about the kinds of things you want [child's name] to learn from playing the game now. When you first started playing the game, were there other kinds of things about numbers you wanted [child's name] to learn about, things that were different from the things you try to teach now? What were they? [The interviewer recorded up to four abandoned goals for later reference.] I want you to look at this chart. If you had to give a number between one and seven, and one stands for giving [child's name] little help, and seven stands for giving [child's name] a lot of help, how much help would you say you give [child's name] for learning about [first abandoned goal] when you first started the game *x* months ago? Why this number? [This line of questioning was completed for each of the mother's stated goals.]

Future Play

Description of Projected Play with Activity

I'd like you to consider how you might be doing this activity in a few months from now. Do you think that the way you would do it would change? How do you think you will be playing the game in several months from now? How does that differ from now?

Mothers' Projected Goals and Amount of Projected Assistance

You told me before that you wanted [child's name] to learn [first current goal] now. Do you think this will still be a goal several months from now? [If not,] Why not? [If yes,] How much help do you think you would be giving [child's name] for [first current goal] several months from now? [The mother is presented with the same seven-point scale noted previously.] Why this number? Do you think that there will be new things about numbers that you will want [child's name] to learn from this activity in several months that you have not mentioned? What are they? [The interviewer recorded up to four novel projected goals for later reference.] I want you to look at this chart. If you had to give a number between one and seven, and one stands for giving [child's name] little help, and seven stands for giving [child's name] a lot of help, how much help would you say you will be giving [child's name] for learning about [first novel projected goal] several months from now? Why this number? [This line of questioning was completed for each of the mother's novel projected goals.]

Additional Activities for Achieving Current Goals in Present, Past, and Future

You said that one thing about numbers you want [child's name] to learn is [first current goal]. Are there other ways that you encourage [child's name] to learn about [first current goal] now? What are they? [The interviewer elicited description. This line of questioning was completed for each of the mother's current goals.] When you first introduced or tried to teach [child's name] about [first current goal], how did you do it? [The interviewer elicited descriptions of stated activities.] How long ago was that? Do you think there will be other sorts of activities in the future you may do with [child's name] to help him/her learn about [first current goal]? [The interviewer elicited descriptions of stated activities.]

Precursory Activities and Activities for Which Selected
Activities Are Precursory

Precursors to Selected Activities

We have been talking about your play with [child's name] on
[current activity]. Were there other number activities in the past that
you and [child's name] did that prepared him/her for doing [current
activity]? What were they? [The interviewer elicited descriptions of the
stated activities]. How did they prepare [child's name] for doing
[current activity]?

Selected Activities as Precursors of Projected Activities

Are there other activities that you might be doing in the future with
[child's name] that might build on what he/she has learned about numbers from [current activity]? What are they? [The interviewer elicted
descriptions of stated activities.] What do you hope [child's name] will
learn from these activities?

REFERENCES

Antell, S. E., & Keating, D. P. (1983). Perception of numerical invariance in neonates. *Child Development*, **54**, 695–701.

Baroody, A. J. (1979). *The relationships among the development of counting, number conservation, and basic arithmetic abilities.* Unpublished doctoral dissertation, Cornell University.

Bee, H. L., Van Egeren, L. F., Streissguth, A. P., Nyman, B. A., & Leckie, M. S. (1969). Social class differences in maternal teaching strategies and speech patterns. *Developmental Psychology*, **1**(6), 726–734.

Bernstein, B. (1972). A sociolinguistic approach to socialization, with some reference to educability. In J. Gumperz & D. Hymes (Eds.), *New directions in sociolinguistics* (pp. 465–497). New York: Holt, Rinehart & Winston.

Bradley, R. H., & Caldwell, B. M. (1976). The relation of infants' home environments to mental test performance at fifty-four months: A follow-up study. *Child Development*, **47**, 1172–1174.

Bradley, R., Caldwell, B. M., & Elardo, R. (1977). Home environment, social status, and mental test performance. *Journal of Educational Psychology*, **69**, 697–701.

Briars, D., & Siegler, R. S. (1984). A featural analysis of preschoolers' counting knowledge. *Developmental Psychology*, **20**(4), 607–618.

Brophy, J. E. (1970). Mothers as teachers of their own preschool children: The influence of socioeconomic status and task structure on teaching specificity. *Child Development*, **41**, 79–94.

Brush, L. R. (1978). Preschool children's knowledge of addition and subtraction. *Journal for Research in Mathematics Education*, **9**, 44–54.

Carpenter, T. P., & Moser, J. M. (1982). The development of addition and subtraction problem-solving skills. In T. P. Carpenter, J. M. Moser, & T. A. Romberg (Eds.), *Addition and subtraction: A cognitive perspective* (pp. 9–24). Hillsdale, NJ: Erlbaum.

Carraher, T. N., Carraher, D., & Schliemann, A. (1985). Mathematics in the streets and in the schools. *British Journal of Developmental Psychology*, **3**(1), 21–29.

Coburn, M. (1983). *The effects of empirical counting, developmental level, and set size on children's conservation performance.* Unpublished doctoral dissertation, City University of New York, Graduate Center.

Cohen, W. (1984). *The quantification of number words.* Unpublished doctoral dissertation, City University of New York, Graduate Center.

Dasen, P. R. (1972). Cross-cultural Piagetian research: A summary. *Journal of Cross-cultural Psychology*, **3**(1), 23–39.

Dasen, P. R. (1980). Psychological differentiation and operational development: A cross-cultural link. *Quarterly Newsletter of the Laboratory of Comparative Human Cognition*, **2**(4), 81–86.

Dave, R. H. (1963). *The identification and measurement of environmental process variables that are related to educational achievement.* Unpublished doctoral dissertation, University of Chicago.

Duncan, O. D. (1961). A socioeconomic index for all occupations. In A. J. Reiss, Jr., with O. D. Duncan, P. K. Hatt, & C. C. North, *Occupations and social status* (pp. 109–138). New York: Free Press.

Frege, G. (1884). *Die Grundlagen der Arithmetik.* Breslau: Marcus.

Fuson, K. C. (1982). An analysis of the counting-on solution procedure in addition. In T. P. Carpenter, J. M. Moser, & T. A. Romberg (Eds.), *Addition and subtraction: A cognitive perspective* (pp. 67–81). Hillsdale, NJ: Erlbaum.

Fuson, K. C., & Hall, J. W. (1983). The acquisition of early number word meanings: A conceptual analysis and review. In H. P. Ginsburg (Ed.), *The development of mathematical thinking* (pp. 49–107). New York: Academic Press.

Fuson, K. C., Pergament, G. G., Lyons, B. G., & Hall, J. W. (1985). Children's conformity to the cardinality rule as a function of set size and counting accuracy. *Child Development, 56,* 1429–1436.

Fuson, K. C., Richards, J., & Briars, D. J. (1982). The acquisition and elaboration of the number word sequence. In C. J. Brainerd (Ed.), *Children's logical and mathematical cognition* (Vol. 1, pp. 33–92). New York: Springer-Verlag.

Gelman, R. (1972). The nature and development of early number concepts. In H. W. Reese (Ed.), *Advances in child development* (Vol. 7, pp. 115–167). New York: Academic Press.

Gelman, R., & Gallistel, C. R. (1978). *The child's understanding of number.* Cambridge, MA: Harvard University Press.

Gelman, R., & Meck, E. (1983). Preschoolers' counting: Principles before skill. *Cognition, 13,* 343–359.

Gelman, R., Meck, E., & Merkin, S. (1986). Young children's numerical competence. *Cognitive Development, 1,* 1–29.

Ginsburg, H. P. (1977). *Children's arithmetic: The learning process.* New York: Van Nostrand.

Ginsburg, H. P., & Russell, R. L. (1981). Social class and racial influences on early mathematical thinking. *Monographs of the Society for Research in Child Development, 46*(6, Serial No. 193).

Greeno, J. G., Riley, M. S., & Gelman, R. (1984). Conceptual competence and children's counting. *Cognitive Psychology, 16,* 94–134.

Groen, G. J., & Parkman, J. M. (1972). A chronometric analysis of simple addition. *Psychological Review, 79,* 329–343.

Hess, R. D., & Shipman, V. C. (1965). Early experience and the socialization of cognitive modes in children. *Child Development, 36,* 869–888.

Kamii, M. (1981, May). *Children's ideas about written number.* Paper presented at the eleventh symposium of the Jean Piaget Society, Philadelphia.

Kellaghan, T. (1977). Relationship between home environment and scholastic behavior in a disadvantaged population. *Journal of Educational Psychology, 69,* 754–760.

Kirk, G. E., Hunt, J. McV., & Volkmar, F. (1975). Social class and preschool language skill: 5. Cognitive and semantic mastery of number. *Genetic Psychology Monographs, 92,* 131–135.

Klein, A. (1984). *The early development of arithmetic reasoning: Numerative activities and logical operations.* Unpublished doctoral dissertation, City University of New York, Graduate Center.

Laosa, L. M. (1980). Maternal teaching strategies in Chicano and Anglo-American families: The influence of culture and education on maternal behavior. *Child Development, 51,* 759–765.

133

Lave, J. (1977). Cognitive consequences of traditional apprenticeship training in West Africa. *Anthropology and Education Quarterly,* **8,** 177–180.

Marjoribanks, K. (1972). Environment, social class, and mental abilities. *Journal of Educational Psychology,* **63,** 103–109.

Marjoribanks, K. (1977). Socioeconomic status and its relation to cognitive performance as mediated through the family environment. In A. Oliverio (Ed.), *Genetics, environment, and intelligence* (pp. 385–403). Amsterdam: Elsevier/North Holland Biomedical Press.

Marjoribanks, K. (1979). *Families and their learning environments: An empirical analysis.* Boston: Routledge & Kegan Paul.

Markman, E. M. (1979). Classes and collections: Conceptual organization and numerical abilities. *Cognitive Psychology,* **11,** 395–411.

Mosychuk, H. (1969). *Differential home environments and mental ability patterns.* Unpublished doctoral dissertation, University of Alberta.

Pedhazur, E. J. (1982). *Multiple regression in behavioral research: Explanation and prediction.* New York: Holt, Rinehart & Winston.

Piaget, J. (1952). *The child's conception of number.* New York: Norton.

Piaget, J. (1966). Need and significance of cross-cultural studies in genetic psychology. *International Journal of Psychology,* **1,** 3–13.

Piaget, J. (1970). Piaget's theory. In P. H. Mussen (Ed.), *Carmichal's manual of child psychology* (3d ed., pp. 703–732). New York: Wiley.

Piaget, J. (1975, June). *On correspondences and morphisms.* Paper presented to the Jean Piaget Society, Philadelphia.

Posner, J. (1982). The development of mathematical knowledge in two West African societies. *Child Development,* **53,** 200–208.

Resnick, L. B. (1982). Syntax and semantics in learning to subtract. In T. P. Carpenter, J. M. Moser, & T. A. Romberg (Eds.), *Addition and subtraction: A cognitive perspective* (pp. 136–155). Hillsdale, NJ: Erlbaum.

Rogoff, B., Ellis, S., & Gardner, W. (1984). The adjustment of adult-child instruction according to child's age and task. *Developmental Psychology,* **20**(2), 193–199.

Rogoff, B., & Gardner, W. P. (1981, March). *Developing cognitive skills in social interaction.* Paper presented to the Society for Research in Child Development study group on "Everyday Cognition: Its Development in Social Context," Laguna Beach, CA.

Saxe, G. B. (1977). A developmental analysis of notational counting. *Child Development,* **48,** 1512–1520.

Saxe, G. B. (1979). Developmental relations between notational counting and number conservation. *Child Development,* **50,** 180–187.

Saxe, G. B. (1981). Body parts as numerals: A developmental analysis of numeration among the Oksapmin in Papua New Guinea. *Child Development,* **52,** 306–316.

Saxe, G. B. (1983). Culture, counting, and number conservation. *International Journal of Psychology,* **18,** 313–318.

Saxe, G. B. (1985). Effects of schooling on arithmetical understandings: Studies with Oksapmin children in Papua New Guinea. *Journal of Educational Psychology,* **77**(5), 503–513.

Saxe, G. B. (1987, April). *Cognition in context: Studies with Brazilian child candy sellers.* Paper presented at the 1987 bienniel meeting of the Society for Research in Child Development, Baltimore.

Saxe, G. B., Gearhart, M., & Guberman, S. R. (1984). The social organization of early number development. In B. Rogoff & J. V. Wertsch (Eds.), *Children's learning in the "zone of proximal development"* (New Directions for Child Development, Vol. **23,** pp. 19–30). San Francisco: Jossey-Bass.

Saxe, G. B., & Mastergeorge, A. (1986). *A developmental analysis of children's strategies to compensate for counting errors.* Unpublished manuscript, University of California, Los Angeles.

Saxe, G. B., & Posner, J. (1983). The development of numerical cognition: Cross-cultural perspectives. In H. P. Ginsburg (Ed.), *The development of mathematical thinking* (pp. 291–317). New York: Academic Press.

Saxe, G. B., Sadeghpour, M., & Sicilian, S. (1986). *Developmental differences in children's understanding of number word conventions.* Unpublished manuscript, University of California, Los Angeles.

Schaeffer, B., Eggleston, V. H., & Scott, J. L. (1974). Number development in young children. *Cognitive Psychology,* **6,** 357–379.

Shannon, L. (1978). Spatial strategies in the counting of young children. *Child Development,* **49,** 1212–1215.

Sicilian, S. (1985). *Counting strategies in blind children.* Unpublished doctoral dissertation, City University of New York, Graduate Center.

Siegler, R. S. (1986). *Children's thinking.* Englewood Cliffs, NJ: Prentice-Hall.

Siegler, R. S., & Robinson, M. (1982). The development of numerical understandings. In H. W. Reese & L. P. Lipsitt (Eds.), *Advances in child development and behavior* (Vol. **16,** pp. 241–312). New York: Academic Press.

Starkey, P. (1986, April). *Auditory perception of numerosity by infants.* Paper presented at the International Conference on Infant Studies, Los Angeles.

Starkey, P., & Cooper, R. S. (1980). Perception of numbers by human infants. *Science,* **210,** 1033–1035.

Starkey, P., & Gelman, R. (1982). The development of addition and subtraction abilities prior to formal schooling in arithmetic. In T. P. Carpenter, J. M. Moser, & T. A. Romberg (Eds.), *Addition and subtraction: A cognitive perspective* (pp. 99–116). Hillsdale, NJ: Erlbaum.

Steffe, L. P., Thompson, P. W., & Richards, J. (1982). Children's counting in arithmetical problem solving. In T. P. Carpenter, J. M. Moser, & T. A. Romberg (Eds.), *Addition and subtraction: A cognitive perspective* (pp. 83–97). Hillsdale, NJ: Erlbaum.

Strauss, M. S., & Curtis, L. E. (1981). Infant perception of numerosity. *Child Development,* **52,** 1146–1152.

Van Loosbroek, E., & Smitsman, A. W. (1986, April). *The visual perception of number invariance in infants.* Paper presented at the International Conference on Infant Studies, Los Angeles.

Vygotsky, L. S. (1962). *Thought and language.* Cambridge, MA: MIT Press.

Vygotsky, L. S. (1978). *Mind in society.* Cambridge, MA: Harvard University Press.

Wagner, S. H., & Walters, J. (1982). A longitudinal analysis of early number concepts: From numbers to number. In G. E. Forman (Ed.), *From thought to action: From sensorimotor schemes to symbolic operations* (pp. 137–161). New York: Academic Press.

Werner, H., & Kaplan, B. (1963). *Symbol formation.* New York: Wiley.

Wertsch, J. V. (1979). From social interaction to higher psychological processes: A clarification and application of Vygotsky's theory. *Human Development,* **22,** 1–22.

Wertsch, J. V. (1984). The zone of proximal development: Some conceptual issues. In B. Rogoff & J. V. Wertsch (Eds.), *Children's learning in the "zone of proximal development"* (New Directions for Child Development, Vol. **23,** pp. 7–18). San Francisco: Jossey-Bass.

Wertsch, J. V. (Ed.). (1985). *Culture, communication, and cognition: Vygotskian perspectives.* Cambridge, MA: Harvard University Press.

Wertsch, J. V. (1986). *The social formation of mind: A Vygotskian approach.* Cambridge, MA: Harvard University Press.

Wertsch, J. V., McNamee, G. D., McLane, J. B., & Budwig, N. A. (1980). The adult-child dyad as a problem solving system. *Child Development, 51,* 1215–1221.

White, K. R. (1982). The relation between socioeconomic status and achievement. *Psychological Bulletin, 91,* 461–481.

Whitehead, A. N., & Russell, B. (1927). *Principia mathematica* (Vols. 1–3). Cambridge: Cambridge University Press.

Wilkinson, A. C. (1984). Children's partial knowledge of the cognitive skills of counting. *Cognitive Psychology, 16,* 28–64.

Winer, G. A. (1974). Conservation of different quantities among preschool children. *Child Development, 45,* 839–842.

Wolf, R. M. (1964). *The identification and measurement of environmental process variables related to intelligence.* Unpublished doctoral dissertation, University of Chicago.

Wood, D., Bruner, J. S., & Ross, G. (1976). The role of tutoring in problem solving. *Journal of Child Psychology and Psychiatry, 17,* 89–100.

Wood, D., & Harris, M. (1977). An experiment in psychological intervention. *Prospects, 7*(4), 512–527.

Wood, D., & Middleton, D. (1975). A study of assisted problem-solving. *British Journal of Psychology, 66,* 181–191.

Wood, D., Wood, H., & Middleton, D. (1978). An experimental evaluation of four face-to-face teaching strategies. *International Journal of Behavioral Development, 1,* 131–147.

ACKNOWLEDGMENTS

Various individuals aided in the completion of this project. We are particularly grateful to Ginette Delancshere, who served as computer consultant; Christine Nucci and Barbara Whitehurst, who assisted in data collection; Graciela Imperiale, Caesar Pacifici, and Karen DeCotis, who helped structure the coding schemes and code video- and audiotapes; and Steven Sicilian, Karen Deacon, and Emily Filardo, who aided in an initial pilot study. We are indebted to the Lutheran Elementary School of Bay Ridge, New York, for providing space to house our project. Last, but not least, we appreciate the constructive remarks of the two reviewers who commented on a previous draft of the manuscript.

This research was supported by a grant from the National Institute of Education (G-80-0119). Other funding was obtained from small grants from the Spencer Foundation and from the Academic Research Committee, University of California, Los Angeles. Partial funding for Maryl Gearhart's participation was through a National Institute of Mental Health postdoctoral research fellowship (HD07032) from the Mental Retardation Research Center, Neuropsychiatric Institute, University of California, Los Angeles.

First author's mailing address: Graduate School of Education, University of California, Los Angeles, Los Angeles, CA 90024-1521.

COMMENTARY

THE CULTURAL UNCONSCIOUS AS CONTRIBUTOR TO THE SUPPORTING ENVIRONMENTS FOR COGNITIVE DEVELOPMENT

COMMENTARY BY ROCHEL GELMAN AND CHRISTINE M. MASSEY

This *Monograph*, by Geoffrey B. Saxe, Steven R. Guberman, and Maryl Gearhart, represents a major contribution to our understanding of early numerical abilities. It presents a wealth of data from a large battery of number tasks (or interviews) administered to children and mothers who represent both lower- and middle-class samples. It is especially good to have the data on the common numerical skills of lower- and middle-class 2-year-olds and the related findings on the common educational goals of the two classes of mothers. Saxe et al. also show, with careful analyses of videotaped sessions, that mothers "teach" their charges in the context of a novel number game and do so especially well when their "lessons" build on the child's numerical goals. Hence, the authors conclude that children's numerical goals are very much an integral part of the nature of the environmental input they receive from adults, in this particular case, their mothers.

For us, this *Monograph* raises a deep theoretical issue for all who study cognitive development, be it in the numerical domain or not. As soon as one

Partial support for preparation of this Commentary came from National Science Foundation grant BNS 85-19575 to Rochel Gelman and a National Science Foundation Graduate Fellowship to Christine Massey. We gratefully acknowledge the cooperation and support of the director, Portia Sperr, and the staff of the Please Touch Museum in Philadelphia. We are grateful to the University of Pennsylvania students who did more than take our methods course: they evolved into members of our research team. Melissa Cohen and Kathleen Letizia are especially acknowledged since they worked on the number exhibit discussed here. We also thank Alan Fiske for reading an earlier draft of this Commentary. Requests for reprints should be sent to the authors at the Psychology Department, University of Pennsylvania, 3815 Walnut Street, Philadelphia, PA 19104.

takes the position that children are actively involved in their own cognitive development, the need for a theory of what is and what is not a supporting environment becomes especially noteworthy. This *Monograph* is full of information about the kinds of numerical props that can be found in the young child's environment. Saxe et al. remind us that it offers books, games, rhymes, and toys that both lower- and middle-class parents buy. It also contains adults who can, when asked, articulate a developmental agenda for their children's number skills.

By themselves, these facts about the environment do not guarantee that children will learn numerical concepts. It is one thing for a stimulus to be present in the environment and quite another matter for the novice learner to notice it and then treat it as do those who already treat these props as part of the numerical environment. How one characterizes the learner has consequences for an account of what is a relevant supporting environment. To illustrate, consider one common characterization of the learner. Couched in terms of numerical concepts, the view is that numerical concepts develop as children are reinforced by adults who provide and model the use of the necessary materials, materials they define as relevant. Over time, as a function of amount of experience and reinforcement, children acquire the various component skills that together will build toward an understanding of number.

According to the foregoing account (one that is most readily identified with the association theory of mind), children are simply receivers of the stimuli they are offered. There is no need to speak of them structuring, let alone creating, their own supporting environments. We are sure that Saxe et al. would not approve of this conclusion. As we said, they contend (and show) that children are very much involved in the determination of what adults will try to teach them. For Saxe et al., children are very actively involved in their acquisition of numerical concepts and skills. Indeed, they are seen as taking the lead by setting themselves numerical goals, goals that reflect their level of competence at a given point in development. Adults then respond to the numerical goals children initiate, by both supporting the children's current efforts and trying to move them to a somewhat more advanced goal level. If this negotiation is successful, then the adult succeeds in providing the child with a socially organized experience that is critical in any account of cognitive development insofar as it constitutes the "material" out of which children produce novel cognitive developments.

In sum, this *Monograph* develops the view that cognitive development is a process of negotiation between the child's own goals and a guiding adult who takes these into account. Environments do not simply impress themselves on the child because the child determines her own numerical goals and does so as a function of her level of competence. If the environment made available is not suited to this goal, it will, presumably, be ignored.

Readers will recognize the foregoing argument as a variant of the Vygotskiian account of cognitive development, a similarity clearly acknowledged, indeed sought after, by the authors. Insofar as it gives children a central role in their own cognitive development, it also overlaps with both the Piagetian and our account of cognitive development. As Liben (1987) notes, our general position (Gelman, 1986) is very close to Piaget's. Although we grant more initial competence, we share Piaget's view of the child as self-motivator and self-generator of activities that lead her to find and use appropriate supporting environments. Thus, like Saxe et al., we too characterize children's numerical activities in terms of goals they set. Our analysis of the variables that contribute to their goals includes social as well as nonsocial context factors, such as the nature of the talk between the child and others in the setting, the nature of the props that are provided or need to be found, and the extent to which children have developed an understanding of the mathematical meaning of terms. In fact, we argue that the acquisition of mature mathematical concepts is very much dependent on the development of symbolic representations that stand for the implicit numerical knowledge young children have (see esp. Gelman & Greeno, in press; and Gelman & Meck, 1986).

As compared to Saxe et al., we are inclined to place even more control of early cognitive development, and hence the definition of supporting environments, in the hands of the children. We assume that young children are motivated to develop further mathematical competence for much the same reasons Piagetians contend they are. Available structures are taken to be self-motivating. Thus, individuals actively pursue and even create environments that can support the development of available structures—even if they do not encounter the competent adult teacher so well characterized by Saxe et al.

It is not that we think that mathematical concept development can proceed without a supporting environment or that this environment is not social. At some level of description, almost anything we might treat as a supporting environment for the development of number concepts is social in nature. This follows from the fact that, with development, children acquire the conventionalized mathematical symbol system. There would be no sense to make of the idea that numerical symbol systems are conventional if they were not shared by, and did not communicate between, people. But this characterization of the environment as social is very different from one that holds that adults have to package it as a function of the child's level of competence. It is simply a statement that transmission of numerical knowledge, by whatever means, involves the transmission of the meaning of mathematical language and its rules of usage. For development to proceed then, there must be examples of the language and its use in the culture. How one comes to understand the meaning of these examples is a separate question.

An example from a somewhat different domain of cognition, knowledge of visual perspective, helps make this point.

Landau and Gleitman (1985) show, contrary to the assumption of John Locke and many others since him, that congenitally blind children do learn how to use visual terms such as "show," "look up," and "see" correctly. Locke's conclusion that they could not followed from the assumption that it was obvious that the supporting environment for visual concepts is the visual sense data picked up by the eye. But, despite the blind child Kelli's inability to sense the presumed essential visual data, she did learn the meaning of visual terms as evidenced by her ability to face forward when asked, "Show me your face," to turn around when asked, "Show me your back," and to take the difference between transparent and opaque barriers into account when showing things to sighted people. After examining a number of possible environmental sources that could have been used here, Landau and Gleitman arrived at the conclusion that syntactic variables that govern the use rules of these verbs provided some of the necessary input. On a priori grounds, it is not clear that one would expect a young child to use this aspect of the environment to figure out how to interpret this kind of verbal data. That she probably did underscores for us the distance we have to go before we have a satisfactory theory of a supporting environment.

One way to summarize Saxe et al.'s contribution is to say that it starts us down the road toward a theory of the environment. To say that the authors have but started is not to minimize their contribution. For it seems that most do not even realize that a constructivist theory of development alters the standard assumptions about what is or is not part of a supporting environment. What counts as an environment, whether different environments may lead to similar outcomes, and the role of various environmental components in conceptual development in different domains all are issues we believe must now be addressed.

The adult-child negotiated, socially organized experiences of the kind Saxe et al. document are surely candidate supporting environments. But to say they may be one kind of supporting environment is not to say they are *the* supporting environment and therefore necessary inputs. There are two classes of reasons to exercise caution here. First, it is conceivable that other supporting environments will do as well or better. In fact, we believe that it has to be that there are other kinds of environments that can and do suffice. There is the obvious fact that mother-child interactions vary widely across cultures. This is so even in the case of language acquisition, for which it would seem safe to assume that all children will become competent. (For further discussion of this issue, see Schieffelin & Ochs, 1986.) But, even within our own culture, any of a variety of other people (children included) can now catch a young child, so to speak, on the fly and offer food for thought. And it is not only people who serve this function.

Our cultural unconscious is permeated with mathematical artifacts, and children have a potential smorgasbord of supporting props, should they be inclined to seek out mathematically relevant inputs for the various goals they establish. They accompany their parents on shopping trips; hear numbers used in talk about time, birthdays, and how many presents they will or will not get; and ride elevators in buildings with many floors. Long-distance driving and the consequent talk about how far one has gone or has yet to go "to get to grandma's" is not uncommon. They watch the Count on the television program "Sesame Street" talk about his passion for counting different set sizes, or Zorro looking for nothing so he can count zero things, or even a puppet dressed up in a black leather jacket singing "Born to Add" set to the tune of a popular rock and roll song.

The latter examples make the point that findings from the study of cognitive development have found their way into the public domain and dramatically altered the array of props children can find on their own. Similarly, developments in the history of mathematics have made their way from discovery to standard availability. Ponder how different things are since Peyps's days, when one went to university to learn to do long division. And it was not that long ago when different units served those who measured length, cloth, land, and so on. Now we take a common unit of length and the long division algorithm for granted. We even take it as given that these should be taught in the first 4 years of elementary school.

There have been more recent changes in our mathematical cultural unconscious. It was only 20 years ago that those who study cognitive development denied the preschooler any arithmetic prowess at all. Who could anticipate the current debate as to whether we should offer formal instruction in the preschool years? But, more important, since even those who studied the numerical abilities of preschoolers talked mainly about the absence of these, it is unlikely that we were also participating in negotiated, mathematically meaningful goal structures. Yet, those early studies replicated. Somehow the children were using their environment to get the intellectual nourishment they needed.

Karmiloff-Smith and Inhelder's (1974/1975) description of block balancing as well as the DeLoache, Sugarman, & Brown (1985) accounts of stacking cup behavior provide particularly compelling cases for the idea that children are self-motivated to change their interpretation of the self-same environmental prop. As they do so, their use of the materials reveals a developmental progression of their understanding of the conceptual domain the materials serve. Environments can also be creations (or logical experiences, in Piagetian terms) generated by the mind from existing mental structures, as when children set themselves the task of counting as high as they possibly can. From interviews with children as young as 5, we know that some children even conclude, on their own, that they need never stop counting and so there cannot be an end to the numbers. It is hard to forget the 4-year-old who said she was not ready to leave the playground to participate in one of our ongoing research projects. Even though she seemed to be doing nothing, she reported that she was "busy counting to a million." When asked when she would be ready, she said she was not sure because she had been counting for a very long time already and had not gotten all that far.

That children in our culture can sample and impose their own interpretations on the rich mathematical environment is one reason we are impressed with how hard it is to follow Saxe et al. in their pursuit of a theory of a supporting environment for those who help construct their own knowledge. Additionally, the very adults who are competent to serve as members of negotiated learning interludes may not reveal this competence in all settings and for all domains. Whether adults in our culture behave with their children as mothers did in the Saxe et al. studies could depend very much on the setting they and their charges find themselves in (cf. Laboratory of Comparative Human Cognition, 1983). We develop this point by sharing some preliminary findings on the way adults and children use a museum that specializes in exhibits for children.

Philadelphia offers young children the Please Touch Museum, which is designed for children younger than 7 years of age. Since the museum's clients are too young to be on their own, the community assumes that this is a place where children visit either in school groups (during the weekday mornings) or with one or two parents (caretakers). The latter is the norm on weekday afternoons and during the weekends. The contents of the museum are what one might expect given a staff who specialize in the culture of the preschooler. There one finds what we classify as *skill-oriented* exhibits (e.g., blocks, puzzles); *sociocultural* exhibits (e.g., a grocery store, a health center with medical equipment and displays, and an old-fashioned trolley), *fantasy exhibits* (e.g., dress up, be in the circus, be in a puppet show), and *more formal learning activities* (e.g., a variety of items for learning about physical mechanisms, a number exhibit, a sound calliope, and live animals). Additionally, considerable care is taken to present the social history of toys, either through the medium of special display items or by the inclusion of toys from the "olden days." From our point of view, this particular setting offers a wide variety of instantiations of what our society's cultural unconscious contains as it bears on the interests preschool-aged children either do or should have.

Our notion that number-relevant materials have achieved this status is reinforced by the very fact that the museum staff developed a number exhibit, called "1-2-3-Go!" Although we read scripts and edited staff-prepared materials for parents and children, we did not develop the "1-2-3-Go!" exhibit. Our plan to observe the use of the exhibit developed 2 years later, when we taught a laboratory class and the museum served as the research setting. That many of the displays in the exhibit offered many of the numerical goals studied by Saxe et al. reflects the staff's general view that they should base their exhibits on what is taken as known and not on what one group of basic researchers might choose. There were displays for constructing and comparing sets, ordering, finding numerals, creating a given cardinal value, counting, and so on—a virtual feast from the number world of the preschool literature.

It is important to us that this exhibit was but one of many that children and adults could visit. Surely, readers will have wondered how many of the Saxe et al. interaction data can be attributed to the fact that neither adult nor child had a choice of other activities. Both child and adult were watched or interviewed in a setting in which numerical activities and goals clearly set the agenda. Would adults, who were competent as "teachers" in the reported studies, do the same things if they were not specifically set to think about the similar materials as numerically relevant ones—if they could wander off to talk to another adult, if they could sit down on a nearby bench and read as they monitored their children, and so on? Similarly, the nature of the child-adult interaction could be influenced by whether the child knows there is anything else to do. It may be that research that targets only one shareable activity is problematic for those who seek an account of the causal relations between children's skeletal competences and the environments that support the development of these. For, in doing this, it makes explicit to the participants the goal of the study (i.e., the nature and quality of adult-child interactions, how to structure use of materials, etc.). It also limits what adults take to be an important social right, to choose their partners and settings depending on what goal they want to achieve. If so, what are we to make of the idea that numerical concept development requires the kind of negotiated shared interactions Saxe et al. study? To repeat, it is one thing to find that such interactions occur in a given setting or set of settings and quite another to assume that they are required or common enough to account for the acquisition in question.

There are well-known pitfalls of the kind of research we have been doing in the museum (see, e.g., Altman, 1974; Garfinkle, 1967; Lofland & Lofland, 1984). First and foremost is the concern that we will stand out as nonmuseum people and therefore cause a change in the very behaviors we want to watch (Goffman, 1974). Several factors helped us become participant observers. Staff and volunteers constitute a legitimate sample of adults who can be in the museum unaccompanied by a young child. We were especially fortunate to have a staff willing to help us get to the point where we could "pass" (Goffman, 1963). We all either had or were given museum titles and badges to so identify ourselves. Similar badges identify all adult nonvisitors, whether personnel or volunteers on the floor. Staff offered their space for the class meetings at the museum and often sat in on them. They shared what they knew as we talked freely about what we were seeing and doing. Before any focused observations were started, we spent a lot of time simply being on the floor, often while counting the distribution of people at the various exhibits (see below). Counts occurred at fixed times; otherwise, we did what others with our title might do on the floor, including answering adults' questions, helping children, and so on. All these activities added to our participant status (museum personnel are always counting something). More important, they offered a chance to watch and garner hypotheses about the use of the museum. If we were at the museum together, we would gather somewhere away from the main exhibit floor and simply talk and take notes. (We did not allow ourselves the use of electronic recorders for this kind of activity, and we agreed to do counts that sampled floor use at different times of the day and on different days, including weekends.) After more than a month of this kind of activity, we started to focus on areas of interest, doing so separately or in pairs. This generated hypotheses about the activities that took place at the chosen site, what to code in terms of interaction variables, and what conditions (if any) to vary. Finally, after about 2½ months serving as participant observers, some detailed observations of a few limited sites—including the number exhibit— were made. The positions of observers were selected so as to be out of the main flow of activity and yet to provide a clear line of sight. If tape recording seemed necessary, the equipment was placed inside or under an item in the target setting.

To summarize, our observations were of three kinds: (1) simple counts of the distribution of children and adults at the different areas on the floor, as function of time of day (morning or afternoon), section of the week (weekday or weekend), and sex (in all, we collected over 40 separate counts); (2) the kind of activity type (or, in Saxe et al.'s terms, goal) on a given item or exhibit; and (3) the degree and nature of child-adult interactions on an item or a display.

Since school groups can make reservations during weekday mornings, adult-child interaction patterns are of two kinds. Morning visits are made by both school groups and dyads of child and adult. During weekday afternoons and all day on weekends, the norm is a dyad of one child and one adult. For example, weekend counts taken in the winter and early spring yielded adult-child ratios of 1.00 and 1.02. For obvious reasons, the morning weekday ratios are never this high. Whenever we counted, the ratio of boys to girls was either 1.0 or very nearly so. In contrast, adult women far outnumber adult men during the week. The weekend female-male adult ratios, taken at the same time as the above child ones, were 1.1 and 1.2, indicating a slight tendency for women to outnumber men.

To get general levels of interest in the different sites at the museum, we divided the floor into 10 areas so that all display areas were covered and yet the people we had to count could be seen clearly. No matter how we analyze these counts, the number exhibit was very popular for everyone. Once differences in overall attendance baseline rates are adjusted, we find little in the way of consistent sex or age differences in attendance rates at the different viewing areas in the afternoon or on weekends. Focusing on the weekend sample, when both children and adults of both sexes were present, we determined that the "1-2-3-Go!" exhibit area was the second most popular for both adults and children. The most popular area for the children included several different displays: a somewhat scaled-down, but otherwise realistic, trolley car; a table with gears and dominoes (in the spring) or inclined planes (in the winter); a full-sized telephone booth; and an old-fashioned kitchen, equipped with actual pre-1900 items. This complex was adjacent to the area adults favored, one that provides a lot of comfortable places to sit and watch a somewhat protected tot area, to visit with others, and to monitor the trolley and grocery store areas.

The primary focus of our intensive observations in the "1-2-3-Go!" exhibit was a display titled "How Many?" It consisted of a freestanding cube, approximately 3 feet high, 2 feet wide, and 2 feet deep. Each of the four vertical faces contained six red doors, each of which could be lifted by a knob to reveal a picture underneath. At the top of each face of the exhibit was the phrase "How many . . ." in large bold letters. A completion of the question for each picture was written across the door covering the picture. For example, a door covering a photograph of a car might ask, "How many headlights on a car?" while the question accompanying a photograph of a building might ask, "How many windows on this building?" Almost all the set sizes represented varied from two to 10; two pictures portrayed 12 items (e.g., eggs in an egg carton) and one more than 30 (the petals on a daisy). Thus, appropriate interaction with this exhibit approximates some of the tasks in Saxe et al.'s study by asking visitors to count and determine cardinal values for sets of various sizes.

Although the age range is broader in our museum sample, the age distribution overlaps with the sample in this *Monograph*. Specifically, three museum subjects were younger than 2 years, 16 were 2 years old, seven were 3 years old, 15 were 4 years old, 12 were 5 years old, six were 6 years old, and one was 7 years old. (For children attending the museum in groups, the ages were usually known. In other cases, the observers estimated the children's ages. To check the accuracy of their estimations, they asked some of the adults, at the end of the observation period, the age of the children with them.) Subjects in the museum during the times of the focused number observations were predominantly middle class. Thus, our museum observations were based on a sample that overlapped Saxe et al.'s middle-class samples. Additionally, our observations were made in the context of a task much like that Saxe et al. used when they videotaped mother-child interactions. So, despite the quite different circumstances, we think there is enough overlap to make the comparison informative.

Two independent observers recorded data in a series of observation periods planned to take place within a given time frame but at different times of day and on different days of the week. Morning sessions were oversampled with a view to observing as many children who did not go to the museum with their parents as possible. The first child (and accompanying adult, if any) to enter the area during these times was the first observed. As soon as the data collection was completed for that subject, the next child to approach the exhibit plus any adults accompanying that child served as the subject for the next set of observations. Seventeen children were observed by themselves at the target exhibit; 43 children were observed in the company of an adult. Observers used a data sheet already marked with a hierarchy of behaviors. The hierarchy was developed by the observers at an earlier time and represented increasingly intensive interactions with the display, ranging from merely opening the doors and looking at the pictures, to labeling and pointing at them, to counting, counting correctly, completing a count, and stating a cardinal value for a set. In addition, records were kept of when an adult asked a "how many" question for a picture, requested the child to count, or praised the child.

Of the 43 adults observed, 13 did not interact at all with either the display or the child; the children with them never did more than open the doors and look at the pictures. As a matter of fact, children who visited the exhibit by themselves were more likely than the children accompanied by a noninteracting adult at least to point and label the pictures, though none counted—even though they were, on the average, 4 years old and, therefore, overlapped with Saxe et al.'s 4-year-old group. To us, the most surprising result is how little numerical behavior, on the part of either children or adults, took place at this display. Of the 30 adults who did interact with the children, only 14 asked a "how many" question, and only eight either counted, requested the child to count, or stated a cardinal value. Only six of the 60 children engaged in any sort of counting, and only five children stated a cardinal value for at least one of the sets. Children who were accompanied by an adult who either engaged in numerical behavior or encouraged the child to do so were significantly more likely to count and to exhibit cardinality. But a substantial majority of the adults observed did neither.

Given that so few adults participated at a level that encouraged numerical thinking in the young children they were with, we have to question whether the kinds of adult-child interactions described in this *Monograph* are common enough outside of an experimental setting to serve as a primary source for children's conceptual development in this domain. It startled us

147

that the adults did not even read the very large sign that said "How many . . ." to their children. These children were, after all, preliterate and needed someone to read the sign for them if they were to know what goal the museum wanted them to set when using the exhibit. By simply reading the sign, adults could at least support the child's use of the material by letting them know the role the setting was meant to serve. Although we knew that adults often fail to read signs in museums for themselves and older children (e.g., Borun, 1979), we still were not prepared for so many of them to ignore a sign painted in large print right on the display itself that they surely knew none of their charges could read.

Why do the adults do so little to encourage numerical thinking in an attractive setting designed to encourage counting? We can only offer some guesses. Recall that parents preferred what we call the tots area. In fact, their next most preferred areas after the number exhibit shared what we see is an essential feature—a place to sit down and both socialize with other adults and monitor their children. This will not be surprising to those who study the functions museums serve. They are seen variously as places to go to get out of the rain or meet a friend, excuses for a family outing, places to have fun and buy things or eat unusual things, places to watch other people, and places to see things that are not familiar (e.g., Alt & Shaw, 1984; Diamond, 1981). Our informal conversations with adult visitors to the Please Touch Museum support these findings. We have heard that they think of the museum as a kind of park, a bigger and better living room than they have at home, as well as a nice place to bring their young charges.

But this cannot be the whole story, for it is clear that parents do teach in some, if not all, settings at the museum. We have seen a lot of label teaching in the tot area. Additionally, we have seen a very interesting kind of teaching in the grocery store and health center areas, a kind that resembles the parent-as-teacher model that Saxe et al. outline. Here, adults seem to stand by, often on the side, and watch their children role play shopper, clerk, nurse, doctor, sick child, and so on. If matters are proceeding smoothly, children seem to be left pretty much alone. However, when a child does something that is not standard or when the child encounters a novel item, the adult standing by is quick to provide the pertinent input. For example, the grocery store is more like a corner Mom and Pop store than a supermarket, and it has a real cash register, albeit a vintage one. We have come to know that the child on the cash register predictably will check others out by first doing something that looks rather bizarre to an adult—this is to slide a to-be-sold item across the front drawer or top of the register. With a little reflection about children's actual grocery shopping experience, one realizes the child is doing what a clerk at a supermarket does who has an automatic scanner to read the computer-marked prices on most of the items in the store. For the children, checking out groceries involves scanning the object, whether it is marked for this purpose or not and even when no such device is present. That they assume this helps make our point that our culture is full of props that children employ, unbeknownst to the adults who use them, to learn about number-relevant domains. But more to the point here, their action is so salient that it invariably leads the adult, who has simply been watching, to say something. That "something" can be a lesson in social history or one about the difference between corner grocery stores and supermarkets. Similarly, adults "teach" their charges about the X-rays and wheel chairs in the medical center. If detailed observations bear these preliminary ones out, we have one possible account of why the same adults treat the various exhibits so differently.

All normal adults are, in fact, experts on the socio-politico-economic roles their culture expects them to share. Competent adults in our society are expected to have the requisite skills for shopping, going to the doctor, using local transportation, and so on (Edgerton, 1967). In contrast, adults are not presumed to be experts in mathematics, physics, or how to read. Related to this difference is the fact that we assign different teaching functions to different adults. Parents are expected to socialize their children regarding everyday interactions like going to the store and taking the trolley. By and large, we pay teachers to teach math, reading, and other "school subjects." So, even though we might be competent to serve in the latter role, we have an option not to do so. In contrast, we have much less of an option regarding the teaching of daily scripts of interaction.

Might the differences between the Saxe et al. data and our observations reflect this difference in options? In this regard, we draw attention to Greenfield's (1984) finding that Zinacanteco women scaffold their input as a function of the novice weaver's level of knowledge. Greenfield's notion of scaffolding is much like the Saxe et al. one of negotiated goal setting. Her results fit our conjecture that a parent's teaching style might well resemble the one described by Saxe et al. when the content domain in question is one in which the parents do think of themselves as the experts.

We should not rule out the possibility that our observations are due in part to some adults accepting the media's argument that we are an illiterate population with regards to math and science. If so, why not leave the use of a number environment to others to teach even the simplest of numerical concepts? An alternative account of the observed difference is that the adults know how very simple the math is that is represented in the display. So they assume that it is already known. Since there are other ways their children can find to use the display, why not let them do so? Or perhaps the adults think that numbers are work and museums are for play? Conceivably, they do not even realize that they are in a number exhibit. Merkin's (1986) exit interviews of museum patrons lend some credence to all these possibilities. This brings us once again to our major point.

The unstated premise of the above considerations is that learning in different domains might require or tolerate different kinds of supporting environments and that parents are more or less comfortable as tutors for these different domains. If so, it follows that all domains are not equal. If we are right that domains do differ as to what inputs yield learning about them, this has to be a variable in any theory of a supporting environment. Basically, we still know very little about the variables that make up a supporting environment for cognitive development. Readers who are interested in this issue will find some clues in a related literature, that on the nature and effect of mother-child language interactions (e.g., Gleitman & Wanner, 1982; Nelson, 1985; Pinker, 1984; Snow & Ferguson, 1977). The account will surely benefit from analyses that let children give us the clues here. We should be looking for more cases of making up price scanners when none are present or turning to the syntactic rules for verbs of seeing when their eyes fail them if we are even to know how to catalog this thing called a potentially supporting environment. The data that Saxe et al. have collected surely help. Without them, we would know even less about the class of inputs to which children bring their interests and self-generated goals.

Environments offer more than social interactions and an opportunity to develop a shared symbol system. They offer many different institutions and artifacts and a cultural unconscious that children will come to share and use to support and develop their burgeoning cognitive abilities. Sometimes, they will benefit from the fact that adults have the competence described by the authors of this *Monograph*. But they surely cannot depend on it. For the same adults have other interests, interests that might well take over when other adults are present, when they and the children can choose among a variety of goals and materials. The same adults cannot be all things at once. Finally, adults in the same roles in different societies may not share our cultural unconscious, and, hence, their children must look elsewhere for supporting inputs (Atran & Sperber, 1987). Everything points to the requirement that, whatever our classification scheme turns out to be, it will have to have redundant cases of supporting materials for a given domain. A theory of supporting environments for cognitive development must eventually evaluate what environments yield what kinds of conceptual growth and whether environments that take different forms and serve different learning paths may nevertheless lead to equivalent developmental outcomes.

References

Alt, M. B., & Shaw, K. M. (1984). Characteristics of ideal museum exhibits. *British Journal of Psychology*, **75**, 25–36.

Altman, J. (1974). Observational study of behavior: Sampling methods. *Behaviour*, **49**(3–4), 227–267.

Atran, S., & Sperber, D. (1987, June). *Learning without teaching: Its place in culture.* Paper presented to the Fourth Annual Workshop on Culture, Schooling, and Psychological Development, Tel Aviv University, Tel Aviv.

Borun, M. (1979). *Select-a-label: A model computer based interpretive system for science museums.* Philadelphia: Franklin Institute.

DeLoache, J. S., Sugarman, S., & Brown, A. L. (1985). The development of error correction in young children's manipulative play. *Child Development,* **56,** 928–939.

Diamond, J. (1981). *The ethology of teaching: A perspective from the observation of families in science centers.* Unpublished doctoral dissertation, University of California, Berkeley.

Edgerton, R. B. (1967). *The cloak of competence.* Berkeley: University of California Press.

Garfinkle, H. (1967). *Studies in ethnomethodology.* Englewood Cliffs, NJ: Prentice-Hall.

Gelman, R. (1986). First principles for structuring acquisition [Presidential address to Division 7 of the American Psychological Association]. *Newsletter of Division 7, APA* (Fall), pp. 24–38.

Gelman, R., & Greeno, J. G. (in press). On the nature of competence: Principles for understanding in a domain. In L. B. Resnick (Ed.), *Knowing and learning: Issues for a cognitive science of instruction.* Hillsdale, NJ: Erlbaum.

Gelman, R., & Meck, E. (1986). The notion of principle: The case of counting. In J. Hiebert (Ed.), *The relationship between procedural and conceptual competence* (pp. 29–57). Hillsdale, NJ: Erlbaum.

Gleitman, L. R., & Wanner, E. (Eds.). (1982). *Language acquisition: The state of the art.* New York: Cambridge University Press.

Goffman, E. (1963). *Stigma: Notes on the management of spoiled identity.* Englewood Cliffs, NJ: Prentice-Hall.

Goffman, E. (1974). *Frame analysis.* Cambridge, MA: Harvard University Press.

Greenfield, P. M. (1984). A theory of the teacher in the learning activities of everyday life. In B. Rogoff & J. Lave (Eds.), *Everyday cognition* (pp. 117–138). Cambridge, MA: Harvard University Press.

Karmiloff-Smith, A., & Inhelder, B. (1974/1975). If you want to get ahead, get a theory. *Cognition,* **3,** 195–212.

Laboratory of Comparative Human Cognition. (1983). Culture and cognitive development. In W. Kessen (Ed.), *Handbook of child psychology: Vol. 1. History, theory, and methods* (4th ed., pp. 295–356). New York: Wiley.

Landau, B., & Gleitman, L. (1985). *Language and experience: Evidence from the blind child.* Cambridge, MA: Harvard University Press.

Liben, L. S. (1987). Epilogue: Approaches to development and learning: Conflict and congruence. In L. S. Liben (Ed.), *Development and learning: Conflict or congruence?* (pp. 237–252). Hillsdale, NJ: Erlbaum.

Lofland, J., & Lofland, L. H. (1984). *Analyzing social settings.* Davis: University of California, Davis.

Merkin, S. (1986). *An evaluation of Please Touch Museum's 1-2-3-Go! exhibit.* Unpublished report, Please Touch Museum, Philadelphia.

Nelson, K. (1985). *Making sense: The acquisition of shared meaning.* New York: Academic Press.

Pinker, S. (1984). *Language learnability and language development.* Cambridge, MA: MIT Press.

Schieffelin, B. B., & Ochs, E. (1986). Language socialization. *Annual Review of Anthropology,* **15,** 163–191.

Snow, C. E., & Ferguson, C. A. (Eds.). (1977). *Talking to children: Language input and acquisition.* Cambridge: Cambridge University Press.

[**Rochel Gelman** (Ph.D. 1967, University of California, Los Angeles) is professor of psychology at the University of Pennsylvania. She is the author, with C. R. Gallistel, of *The Child's Understanding of Number* (Cambridge, MA: Harvard University Press, 1978). More recent works include "On the Nature of Competence: Principles for Understanding in a Domain," with James G. Greeno, in *Knowing and Learning: Issues for a Cognitive Science of Instruction*, ed. L. Resnick (Hillsdale, NJ: Erlbaum, in press). Her research interests include the development of quantitative and logical concepts, classification, animism, and causality. **Christine M. Massey** is a Ph.D. candidate at the University of Pennsylvania. She is the author, with Rochel Gelman, of "Preschoolers' Ability to Decide Whether a Pictured Unfamiliar Object Can Move Itself," presented at the biennial meeting of the Society for Research in Child Development, Baltimore, April 23–26, 1987. She studies causal reasoning and the development of the distinction between animate and inanimate objects.]

COMMENTARY

SPECIFYING THE DEVELOPMENT OF A COGNITIVE SKILL IN ITS INTERACTIONAL AND CULTURAL CONTEXT

COMMENTARY BY BARBARA ROGOFF

The study of child development has long wrestled with the appropriate characterization of the roles played by nature and nurture, by the child and the environment. For many years, this controversy was cast as a debate between those who argued for nature and those who argued for nurture. Now, as students read in introductory texts, many scholars view both as contributing to human development, with a reconciliation in which the proportion of contribution from each side is sought.

In recent years, however, scholars from a variety of backgrounds have argued that the roles of biology and culture, of the child and the social environment, are complementary and inseparable. They cannot be considered without each other and, indeed, may be seen as different aspects of the phenomenon of development (Brazelton, 1982; Fogel & Thelen, in press; Lancaster, Altmann, Rossi, & Sherrod, 1987; Rogoff, 1982; Vygotsky, 1978; Wartofsky, 1984; Wertsch, 1985). As Als (1979) states, the human newborn is biologically a social organism.

The work of Geoffrey B. Saxe, Steven R. Guberman, and Maryl Gearhart represents a step forward in applying such a perspective to research. This *Monograph* should be influential, not only in its findings, but as an example of how the social and developmental approaches to understanding cognitive development fit together. There is already a vast literature on children's development of cognitive skills, including mathematical concepts, and there is a growing literature on the social contexts of cognitive development. Usually, as Saxe et al. point out, these literatures have paid insufficient attention to each other. The developmental literature may seem to portray the child as a little scientist discovering principles independently, and the socialization literature may give the impression that the child passively soaks up lessons or influence from the environment.

The approach that Saxe et al. find compatible with their own is work they identify as inspired by Vygotsky. They describe their work in this tradition along with that of Bruner, Wood, Wertsch, Rogoff, and collaborators. Vygotsky's theory focuses on social interaction that initiates children to the more mature ways of thinking that have been invented in the history of a society (including number systems, literacy, and mnemonic techniques). Vygotsky introduced the concept of the "zone of proximal development," the sensitive zone where adult-child interaction supports the child in advancing skills beyond the level that could be managed independently by the child. Consistent with Vygotsky's approach, Saxe et al. characterize social interaction in number tasks as negotiations between adult and child, with adults adusting the task organization according to children's needs and children adjusting their goal-directed behavior to the adults' instruction.

As yet, there is little research within this tradition. Existing studies have given interesting accounts of how adults sensitively tailor their instructions or informal interactions with children to the children's age or to their success in performance of a task. This *Monograph* aims to go beyond these studies in several ways: by providing a specified model of children's understanding, by relating performance in particular tasks to the larger sociocultural context, and by attending to children's roles in transforming cultural forms into their own developing understanding.

A Model of Children's Understanding

Saxe et al. point out that the variables of children's age and task success, used in previous research, are not satisfying models of children's capabilities in a task domain. Although their concern that "no study is guided by a model of the child's developing understandings" (p. 59) is an overstatement, their research offers a tremendous step forward in handling this issue. Their analysis of the arithmetic goals that children structure in problem solving and of the relation between these goals and adults' organizing activities provides a sensitive analytic tool for understanding the relation between the child's actions and the adult's assistance and how these fit in the culture's number system.

Use of a model of the goal structures in early understanding of number makes it possible to examine the function of specific supports provided by mothers, from the perspective of their utility to the children. Contrast this approach with one in which adults' assistance is examined in terms of the specificity of help but without determining what help a child needs. If the child's level of understanding is not considered, it is difficult to determine whether specific directives or open-ended suggestions are appropriate. Saxe et al.'s model of the development of number understanding allows assessment of children's skill in handling number problems independently and allows sensitive description of the meshing of adults' assistance with the stumbling points at which the children need assistance. This is the major advance represented by their work.

I would note, however, that although age is a "package variable" (Whiting, 1976) that in itself is not explanatory, it is, nevertheless, a very real variable to adults in our culture. It is one of the first pieces of information that a stranger requests of a child, and it is taken into account in judging the appropriateness of children's skills by parents and teachers. In unpublished analyses, Gardner, Ellis, and I found that mothers' instruction in a memory and classification task related more to the age than to the skills of their children, suggesting that mothers may use age as one way to gauge their instruction.

The Sociocultural Context of Skill

Saxe et al. criticize previous work for not sufficiently examining the larger sociocultural activities in which cognitive tasks fit. They are concerned that isolated activities have been used that are simply assumed to represent an unanalyzed knowledge domain. Presumably, they refer here to the use of puzzle completion, construction, and classification tasks. The authors' use of number-understanding tasks does indeed hold the advantage of ease of relating specific tasks to the larger sociocultural context.

This advantage does not necessarily detract from the use of other tasks in previous research, but it does serve the authors' purpose well. Some of the more interesting findings of this *Monograph* involve the relation between the children's number understandings, the mothers' attempts to assist, and the mothers' reports of the number activities in which children are involved on an everyday basis at home (i.e., the sociocultural level of analysis).

The findings regarding sociocultural arrangements of number learning show that both middle- and working-class preschoolers are heavily involved in number games and activities. This finding challenges assertions that children enter school with a "natural" understanding of number that derives from their own attempts to figure out arithmetic, independent of social influences (e.g., Ginsburg & Allardice, 1984). Long before the onset of formal schooling, these 2- and 4-year-olds are involved in specifically didactic and implicitly informative social activities involving number.

An example is the Clock Game, passed down from one mother's childhood, in which mother and 4-year-old child arrange playing cards according to their value from one to 12 in a clock-face array. This game involved recognition of correspondence between number of figures (e.g., spades) and number symbols, seriation of numbers, and cardinality. The mother described how the nature of the game had changed according to the child's skills (over the 18 months they had been playing) and her plans for expansion to a larger set size using the game of Chutes and Ladders when the child consolidated these skills.

With the rich data set available to the authors, I wish they had included more such individual accounts of what games and activities were played, how they were structured, and how they changed over time. This *Monograph* has an abundance of numbers (fittingly, I suppose), but rich description of some cases would help to give the numbers life and to ground the reader's impressions of what the mothers and children are really doing at home.

A major goal of this *Monograph* is to examine social class differences in children's number skills and the social interaction and social arrangements for children's number learning. Some differences were found between middle- and working-class children's understanding of number, their mothers' aspirations for their educational attainment, and their mothers' instructions (i.e., the complexity of goals that mothers required children to work on). Although these differences make sense and fit with earlier literature, it was surprising to me that there were so few differences—on most analyses, there were no social class differences. I wonder if the subject selection criterion of including only "intact" families made the working-class sample an especially stable subgroup of that population, with more interpersonal resources than may have been available in the lower-class samples of previous investigations.

The Child's Contribution to Socialization

The authors aim to go beyond previous research in giving greater attention to the child's role. They claim that their study examines how children adjust their numerical goals to those required to accomplish the numerical goals that emerge in an interaction. I agree that there is a need to focus on children's role in socialization, and I have argued that the Vygotskian approach has not paid sufficient attention to the child's role as participant in socialization (Rogoff, 1986, in press; Rogoff & Gardner, 1984). My notion of *guided participation* is an attempt to expand the concept of the "zone of proximal development" to include the child as a partner in task analysis and sensitive transmission of information as well as, potentially, the manager of social exchanges. Hence, I applaud the authors' attempt to examine the child's contribution.

In describing what the child brings to the interaction by using a model of number understanding, the authors provide specificity to the child's starting skills. But this *Monograph* falls short of what it could have accomplished through sensitive analyses of what the child contributes to the socialization activities. The primary measure of the child's contribution to socialization is the extent to which the child accepts the mother's help: children perform better with assistance than without (but there is an order confound here), and children adjust to maternal instructions such as requests to count by complying. This work does not provide a very dynamic account of what children do to arrange for learning, in contrast with its excellent investigation of maternal efforts to arrange for learning and sensitivity to the children's level of skill. In future work, I hope the authors will devote similar attention to what children do spontaneously with numbers and what they do to elicit adult assistance in learning.

What Consequences Does Social Interaction Have for Individual Development?

The other major question that goes unanswered in this *Monograph* regards the consequences of social interaction and sociocultural arrangements for children's learning and development. To me, it seems natural for such maternal sensitivity and practice in number games to have an effect on children's learning. This assumption appears to be widely accepted in recent years. However, I think it warrants closer examination. Does social interaction benefit children's later independent performance?

The closest this *Monograph* gets to the question is its analysis of whether children perform better when assisted by mothers than when working independently. (They do.) But in addition to having an order confound, this evidence does not demonstrate that an improvement in performance when working together leads to an improvement in later independent performance. Collaborative performance could be improved because of a mother's taking over the decision making, with no effect or even negative effect on the child's understanding as a result of the collaboration.

We have been too quick to assume blanket effects of social interaction—and so we have not stopped to examine them. My guess is that social interaction will benefit children's learning under some circumstances and not others. The expertise of the partner in the task domain as well as in communication with a novice may be influential. The division of labor in collaborative decision making may lead to very different opportunities for the child to internalize the decision making made in collaboration. For example, if the partner and the child do not think through the problem together but simply divide it up into parts for which they are individually responsible, or if the partner dominates the problem solving without the child being involved enough to follow the expert's thought processes, there may be little benefit from working with another person. Partners may need to establish "intersubjectivity" rather than benefiting from simply being in each other's presence (Gauvain & Rogoff, 1985; Trevarthen & Hubley, 1978; Wertsch, 1984). It is certainly possible for the presence of a partner to have a negative effect if the problem is more easily solved without the distraction of having to handle social negotiation and to externalize a thought process.

Future research is needed to evaluate these speculations that the effects of social interaction depend on the partner having something to offer, the dyad establishing intersubjectivity in decision making, and the task being conducive to shared thinking.

Though Saxe et al. do not address the question of whether and how social interaction and sociocultural arrangements facilitate development, their study provides excellent information on how adults adjust their assistance sensitively to children's level of understanding. They document that children's numerical understanding develops in a rich social context that is structured by the child's current and growing concepts of number. And they provide a model of how the study of social and developmental processes can be merged through sensitive analysis of children's domain understanding and of mothers' adjustments and arrangements of socialization to fit with children's level of understanding.

References

Als, H. (1979). Social interaction: Dynamic matrix for developing behavioral organization. In I. C. Uzgiris (Ed.), *Social interaction and communication during infancy* (pp. 21–39). San Francisco: Jossey-Bass.

Brazelton, T. B. (1982). Joint regulation of neonate-parent behavior. In E. Z. Tronick (Ed.), *Social interchange in infancy* (pp. 7–22). Baltimore: University Park Press.

Fogel, A., & Thelen, E. (in press). Development of early expressive and communicative action: Reinterpreting the evidence from a dynamic systems perspective. *Developmental Psychology.*

Gauvain, M., & Rogoff, B. (1985, April). *The development of planning skills by individuals and dyads.* Paper presented at the meeting of the Society for Research in Child Development, Toronto.

Ginsburg, H. P., & Allardice, B. S. (1984). Children's difficulties in school mathematics. In B. Rogoff & J. Lave (Eds.), *Everyday cognition: Its development in social context* (pp. 194–219). Cambridge, MA: Harvard University Press.

Lancaster, J., Altmann, J., Rossi, A. S., & Sherrod, L. R. (1987). *Parenting across the life span: Biosocial dimensions.* New York: Aldine de Gruyter.

Rogoff, B. (1982). Integrating context and cognitive development. In M. E. Lamb & A. L. Brown (Eds.), *Advances in developmental psychology* (Vol. 2, pp. 125–170). Hillsdale, NJ: Erlbaum.

Rogoff, B. (1986). Adult assistance of children's learning. In T. E. Raphael (Ed.), *The contexts of school based literacy* (pp. 27–42). New York: Random House.

Rogoff, B. (in press). The joint socialization of development by young children and adults. In M. Lewis & S. Feinman (Eds.), *Social influences and behavior.* New York: Plenum.

Rogoff, B., & Gardner, W. P. (1984). Adult guidance in cognitive development. In

B. Rogoff & J. Lave (Eds.), *Everyday cognition: Its development in social context* (pp. 95–116). Cambridge, MA: Harvard University Press.

Trevarthen, C., & Hubley, P. (1978). Secondary intersubjectivity: Confidence, confiding, and acts of meaning in the first year. In A. Lock (Ed.), *Action, gesture, and symbol: The emergence of language* (pp. 183–229). London: Academic Press.

Vygotsky, L. S. (1978). *Mind in society: The development of higher psychological processes.* Cambridge, MA: Harvard University Press.

Wartofsky, M. (1984). The child's construction of the world and the world's construction of the child. In F. S. Kessel & A. W. Siegel (Eds.), *The child and other cultural inventions* (pp. 188–215). New York: Praeger.

Wertsch, J. V. (1984). The zone of proximal development: Some conceptual issues. In B. Rogoff & J. V. Wertsch (Eds.), *Children's learning in the "zone of proximal development"* (pp. 7–18). San Francisco: Jossey-Bass.

Wertsch, J. V. (1985). *Vygotsky and the social formation of mind.* Cambridge, MA: Harvard University Press.

Whiting, B. B. (1976). The problem of the packaged variable. In K. F. Riegel & J. A. Meacham (Eds.), *The developing individual in a changing world.* Chicago: Aldine.

[**Barbara Rogoff** (Ph.D. 1977, Harvard University) is professor of psychology at the University of Utah. Related work includes *Everyday Cognition: Its Development in Social Context*, edited with Jean Lave (Cambridge, MA; Harvard University Press, 1984), and *Children's Learning in the "Zone of Proximal Development,"* edited with James V. Wertsch (San Francisco: Jossey Bass, 1984). Her research focuses on how parents and peers collaborate with children in socializing cognitive development and how development fits in the broader cultural context.]

GOALS AND CONTEXTS

REPLY BY THE AUTHORS

There is much agreement between the *Monograph* and the commentaries. However, at times we believe that aspects of our framework were overlooked as commentators put our work in the context of their own research and analytic approaches. In particular, central to our treatment was a focus on children's goal-directed activities. By focusing on children's goals, we were able to integrate analyses of social and developmental processes in children's understandings. We take this opportunity to bring the reader back to this focus and examine the way it bears on issues raised in the commentaries.

A common focus of the commentaries is the conceptualization of "context" and, more particularly, what counts as a context that promotes cognitive development. Rogoff is herself convinced of the critical status of social interactions in defining contexts and the influence of social interactions on cognitive developmental processes. She points out that interactions are constructed in many different forms, from asymmetrical interactions, in which one participant directs another, to negotiations between equals, and she argues for the need to articulate the implications of these different forms.

Rogoff's sketch makes intuitive sense. We would add that the various types of interactions that Rogoff describes may have different consequences precisely because they have different implications for the *goals* that individuals structure in an activity. For instance, excessive direction by a teacher might restrict opportunities for a learner to construct complex goals, while peer negotiations might permit two learners to construct somewhat novel goals yet limit their complexity. Thus, the analysis that Rogoff points to must be integrated with an analysis of the goal-directed activities of the individual and how those goals are generated and modified in social interactions.

Gelman and Massey take a different tack with regard to the conceptualization of supportive contexts. They argue that didactic interactions involving number games may be only minimally involved as supportive contexts in children's cognitive development, citing as evidence the lack of adult-child interactions in the "1-2-3-Go!" museum exhibit. In their view, children use many different types of contexts to support their developing understandings, contexts that may or may not involve other people directly.

We have no disagreement with Gelman and Massey's concern to understand the multiplicity of contexts in which children's goal-directed activities are influenced and supported by social processes, and, in Chapter V of the *Monograph*, we documented a variety of nondidactic as well as didactic play contexts involving number and solitary as well as social activities. Further, we applaud Gelman and Massey's concern to analyze activities and social interactions in everyday contexts outside teaching interactions, a difficult research endeavor with which we have been engaged in more recent work on mathematical cognition in Brazil (e.g., Guberman, 1987; Saxe, 1987a, 1987b, in press; Saxe & Gearhart, in preparation).

We do not agree, however, with Gelman and Massey's argument against the importance of analyses of didactic interactions in the working- and middle-class communities we sampled. The support for their claim is weak: one should be wary of using negative findings from a single cultural context (such as a museum) to argue for the general lack of occurrence of particular forms of interaction. In Chapter V, we report a good deal of didactic interaction, and, with today's emphasis on early achievement, it is not surprising to observe that parents are initiating interactions and providing activity contexts in which they attempt to "encourage learning and understanding." Researchers should not neglect an analysis of such interactions in a treatment of social processes in cognitive development—interactions in which adults make concerted efforts to influence the character of children's goal-directed activities and in which, as our analyses in Chapters VI and VII show, they have considerable success.

In closing, both commentaries point to the need for richer analyses of children's activities as children address everyday problems in or out of social interactions. The *Monograph* is a step in this direction, one that we hope will serve as a bridge to more comprehensive and theoretically motivated empirical analyses of children's goals and the ways they take form in social life.

References

Guberman, S. R. (1987, April). *Arithmetical problem-solving in commercial transactions of Brazilian children*. Paper presented at the biennial meeting of the Society for Research in Child Development, Baltimore.

Saxe, G. B. (1987a, April). *Cognition in context: Studies with Brazilian candy sellers.* Paper presented at the biennial meeting of the Society for Research in Child Development, Baltimore.

Saxe, G. B. (1987b, July). *The influence of the practice of candy selling on Brazilian children's mathematics.* Paper presented at the meeting of the International Society for Research in Behavioral Development, Tokyo.

Saxe, G. B. (in press). The mathematics of child street venders. *Child Development.*

Saxe, G. B., & Gearhart, M. (in preparation). *Weaving and topological understandings.* University of California, Los Angeles.